THE BELT AND ROAD INITIATIVE

XI JINPING

 FOREIGN LANGUAGES PRESS

First Edition 2019
Third Printing 2019

ISBN 978-7-119-11998-4
© Foreign Languages Press Co. Ltd, Beijing, China, 2019
Published by Foreign Languages Press Co. Ltd
24 Baiwanzhuang Road, Beijing 100037, China
http://www.flp.com.cn
Email: flp@CIPG.org.cn
Distributed by China International Book Trading Corporation
35 Chegongzhuang Xilu, Beijing 100044, China
P.O. Box 399, Beijing, China

Printed in the People's Republic of China

EDITOR'S NOTE

Since the 18th National Congress of the Communist Party of China (CPC), General Secretary Xi Jinping's proposal of the Belt and Road Initiative (BRI) has won a warm welcome from the international community, especially from countries along the routes. One of China's key measures in pursuing all-round opening up in the new era, the initiative serves as an important platform for building a global community of shared future, and providing the world with a solution for common prosperity and development based on Eastern wisdom. Expounding on the guiding principles, rich content, goals, and methods behind the initiative, General Secretary Xi has pointed out the direction for further development, and mapped out a bright future for China. To help readers understand his thoughts on the Belt and Road Initiative and promote international cooperation, the Research Institute of Party History and Literature of the CPC Central Committee and the Office of the Leading Group for the Belt and Road Initiative have jointly compiled *The Belt and Road Initiative*.

This book contains more than 40 speeches and excerpts on the Belt and Road Initiative delivered by Xi between September 2013 and July 2018.

July 2018

CONTENTS

Work Together to
Build the Silk Road Economic Belt[*]

September 7, 2013

More than 2,100 years ago during the Han Dynasty (206 BC-AD 220), a Chinese envoy named Zhang Qian was twice sent to Central Asia on missions of peace and friendship. His journeys opened the door to friendly contacts between China and Central Asian countries, and started the Silk Road linking the East and West, Asia and Europe.

Shaanxi, my home province, is right at the starting point of the ancient Silk Road. Today, as I stand here and look back at history, I seem to hear the camel bells echoing in the mountains and see the wisps of smoke rising from the desert, and this gives me a specially good feeling.

Kazakhstan, located on the ancient Silk Road, has made an important contribution to the exchanges between the Eastern and Western civilizations and the interactions and cooperation between various nations and cultures. This land has borne witness to a steady stream of envoys, caravans,

---

[*] Part of the speech, titled "Promote Friendship Between Our People and Work Together to Build a Bright Future", at Nazarbayev University, Astana, Kazakhstan.

travelers, scholars and artisans traveling between the East and the West. The exchanges and mutual learning thus made possible the progress of human civilization.

The ancient city of Almaty is also on the ancient Silk Road. In Almaty, there is a Xian Xinghai Boulevard, which got its name from a true story. After the outbreak of the Great Patriotic War in 1941, Xian, a renowned Chinese composer, found his way to Almaty. By then, he was worn down by poverty and illness and had no one to turn to. Fortunately, the Kazakh composer Bakhitzhan Baykadamov took care of Xian and provided him with the comfort of a home. It was in Almaty that Xian composed his famous works: *Liberation of the Nation*, *Sacred War* and *Red All over the River*. He also wrote the symphony *Amangeldy* based on the exploits of the Kazakh national hero. These works served as a rallying call to fight Fascism and proved immensely popular with the local people.

Throughout the millennia, the peoples of various countries along the ancient Silk Road have written a chapter of friendship that has been passed on to this very day. More than 2,000 years of exchanges demonstrate that on the basis of unity, mutual trust, equality, inclusiveness, mutual learning and mutually beneficial cooperation, countries of different races, beliefs and cultural backgrounds are fully able to share peace and development. This is the valuable inspiration we have drawn from the ancient Silk Road.

Over the past 20 years, the relations between China and Eurasian countries have grown rapidly, and the ancient Silk

Road has gained new vitality. In a new way, it is lifting the mutually beneficial cooperation between China and Eurasian countries to a fresh height.

Close neighbors are better than distant relatives. China and Central Asian countries are close and friendly neighbors. China values its friendship and cooperation with these countries, and takes improving these relations as a foreign policy priority.

China's relations with the Central Asian countries now face a golden opportunity of growth. We hope to work with these countries to strengthen trust, friendship and cooperation, and promote common development and prosperity to the benefit of all our peoples.

– We should pass on our friendship from generation to generation and remain good neighbors living in harmony. China is committed to peaceful development and an independent foreign policy of peace. We respect the development paths and domestic and foreign policies pursued independently by the people of every country. We will never interfere in the internal affairs of Central Asian countries. We do not seek to dominate regional affairs or establish any sphere of influence. We stand ready to enhance consultation and coordination with Russia and all Central Asian countries to sustain harmony in our region.

– We should firmly support and trust each other and be sincere and good friends. Rendering each other firm support on major issues concerning core interests such as sovereignty, territorial integrity, security and stability underlies China's strategic partnership with the Central Asian countries. We will reinforce trust and cooperation with the Central Asian countries bilaterally and within the framework of the Shanghai Cooperation Organization (SCO) to combat the "three forces" of terrorism, separatism and extremism as well as drug trafficking and organized transnational crimes, and this will create a favorable environment for promoting economic development and improving the wellbeing of the people in this region.

– We should vigorously enhance practical cooperation and be good partners of mutually beneficial cooperation. Both China and the Central Asian countries are at a crucial stage of development, and we face unprecedented opportunities and challenges. We have all set medium- to long-term development goals based on our national conditions. Our strategic goals are the same – to ensure sustainable and stable economic development, build a prosperous and strong nation and achieve national revitalization. Therefore, we need to enhance practical cooperation across the board, use our good political relations, geographical proximity and economic complementarities to boost sustainable growth, and build a community of shared interests and mutual benefit.

– We should expand regional cooperation with a more open mind and broader vision, and achieve joint progress. Global economic integration is accelerating, and regional cooperation is booming. The Eurasian region has a number of regional cooperation organizations. The members and observers of the Eurasian Economic Community (EAEC) and the SCO are from Eurasia, South Asia and West Asia. By intensifying cooperation between the SCO and the EAEC, we will create further space for development.

To forge closer economic ties, deepen cooperation and expand development space in the Eurasian region, we should take an innovative approach and jointly build an economic belt along the Silk Road. This will be a great undertaking benefitting the people of all countries along the routes. To turn this vision into reality, we may start in specific areas and connect them over time to cover the whole region.

First, we need to step up policy consultation. Countries should have full discussions on development strategies and policies, adopt plans and measures for advancing regional cooperation through consultation in the spirit of seeking common ground while setting aside differences, and give the policy and legal "green light" to regional economic integration.

Second, we need to improve road connections. The SCO is working on an agreement on transport facilitation. Its early signing and implementation will open up a major transport route connecting the Pacific and the Baltic. On this basis, we can actively discuss the best way to improve cross-border transport infrastructure and work towards a transport network connecting East Asia, West Asia and South Asia to facilitate economic development and travel in the region.

Third, we need to promote unimpeded trade. The envisaged economic belt along the Silk Road is inhabited by nearly three billion people and it represents the biggest market in the world, with enormous, unparalleled potential for trade and investment cooperation between the countries involved. We should discuss a proper arrangement for trade and investment facilitation, remove trade barriers, reduce trade and investment costs, increase the speed and raise the quality of regional economic flows and achieve mutually beneficial progress in the region.

Fourth, we need to enhance monetary circulation. China and Russia already have sound cooperation on settling trade in local currencies, and have made good progress and yielded rich experience in this respect. This good practice can be shared with others in the region. If our region can realize local currency convertibility and settlement under the current and capital accounts, it will significantly lower circulation cost, increase our ability to fend off financial risks, and make our region more competitive internationally.

Fifth, we need to increase understanding between our peoples. Friendship between peoples is the key to good relations between states. To pursue productive cooperation in the above-mentioned areas, we need the support of our peoples. We should encourage more friendly exchanges between our peoples to enhance mutual understanding and traditional friendship, and build strong public support and a solid social foundation for regional cooperation.

Carry Forward the "Shanghai Spirit" and Promote Common Development*

September 13, 2013

Your Excellency President Almazbek Atambayev,
Dear colleagues,

It gives me great pleasure to attend the Bishkek Summit of the Shanghai Cooperation Organization. I would like to thank Kyrgyzstan, the SCO Presidency, for your meticulous preparations and thoughtful arrangements for the success of this summit. China commends Kyrgyzstan for your enormous and effective efforts over the past year for the SCO's development.

In light of the latest developments in the international and regional situation and in response to the common aspirations of member states for stability, growth and better lives for their peoples, this summit has focused on the implementation of the Treaty of Long-term Good-neighborliness, Friendship and Cooperation. It will ratify the Plan of Action of the Treaty and map out the blueprint for the development of the SCO in the next five years. These efforts will

---

* Speech at the 13th meeting of the Council of Heads of Member States of the Shanghai Cooperation Organization in Bishkek, Kyrgyzstan.

offer broader prospects for the organization.

Just as the SCO enjoys precious opportunities for development, it also faces severe challenges. The "three forces" of terrorism, separatism and extremism all pose threats to the security and stability of this region as do drug trafficking and transnational organized crime. The international financial crisis has caused varying degrees of economic difficulties for countries in this region, leaving them in a period of adjustment and recovery.

Challenges such as these are more than any one country can handle alone. We must therefore enhance cooperation and unite to become stronger. And in this regard, I would like to suggest that we do the following:

First, we should carry forward the "Shanghai Spirit". To implement the "Shanghai Spirit", we should build up trust among member states and conduct mutually beneficial cooperation based on equality, consultation, mutual understanding and mutual accommodation. This conforms to the trend of peace and development of the times and accords with the interests and aspirations of the people of the member states.

We should implement the Treaty of Long-term Good-neighborliness, Friendship and Cooperation with real actions and promote cooperation wholeheartedly in all fields within the SCO framework, so that member states will become good neighbors living in harmony, good friends pulling together in troubled waters and good partners sharing weal and woe.

Second, we should jointly safeguard regional security and

stability. A secure and stable environment is a prerequisite for mutually beneficial cooperation, and common development and prosperity. We should implement the Shanghai Convention on Combating Terrorism, Separatism and Extremism and the Program of Cooperation, improve the system of law enforcement and security cooperation of the SCO, entrust the regional counter-terrorism structure with responsibility for anti-narcotics operations, and on this basis establish a center for comprehensive responses to security threats and challenges.

The relevant authorities within the member states should also open up a channel for routine communication, and explore ways to act and work together to combat terrorism, separatism and extremism so as to create a sound working and living environment for the peoples of this region.

Afghanistan is an observer of the SCO, and its situation is closely related to regional security and stability. The SCO should support it in national reconciliation, help it realize peace and stability as soon as possible, and safeguard regional security.

Third, we should focus on practical cooperation. This is the material basis and main driver for the SCO's development. All the six member states and the five observers are located along the routes of the ancient Silk Road. As such, we are all duty-bound to carry forward the Silk Road spirit by taking the following steps:

Number one, open up new transport and logistics routes. The member states could move speedily to sign the Agreement on the Facilitation of International Road Transport. Once signed, the agreement would be open for wide observer participation on a voluntary basis so that the participating countries could build unimpeded transport corridors connecting the Baltic with the Pacific and connecting Central Asia with both the Indian Ocean and the Persian Gulf.

Number two, explore a trade and investment facilitation agreement. Extensive trade and investment cooperation with full consideration for the interests and concerns of all parties would allow us to thoroughly unlock the potential for cooperation among member states and achieve mutual complementarity in the interest of our common development and prosperity.

Number three, step up cooperation in the financial sector. We should establish an SCO development bank which would provide funding guarantees and serve as a settlement platform for the organization's infrastructure development and collaborative economic and trade projects. In the meantime, the SCO should set up a special account to ensure funding for project studies, exchanges and training within its framework. We should make full use of the inter-bank consortium to intensify exchanges and cooperation between financial institutions of the countries in this region.

Number four, establish an energy club. This would help us coordinate energy cooperation within the SCO framework, secure stable supply and demand, ensure energy security, and, on top of these, encourage extensive cooperation in such areas as energy efficiency and new energy sources.

Number five, put in place a cooperation mechanism for food security. We should enhance cooperation in agricultural production, agrotrade and food safety to ensure greater food security.

Last but not least, we should intensify people-to-people and cultural exchanges to build strong public support and a social foundation for the SCO's future development. We should promote cooperation in a wide range of areas such as culture, education, film and TV, health, sports and tourism.

At the Beijing Summit, China announced a ten-year program of 30,000 government scholarships for the other member states. We are ready to work closely with the other member states to maximize the benefit of this program.

China will also establish a China-SCO base for international judicial exchanges, cooperation and training at Shanghai University of Political Science and Law. We would like to make it a platform for training judicial professionals for other member states.

Traditional medicine is a new area of cooperation. China stands ready to join hands with other member states in building medical institutions specializing in traditional Chinese medicine to make full use of such resources for the benefit of the people of our member states.

China has taken the lead in establishing an SCO Committee on Good-neighborliness, Friendship and Cooperation in line with a consensus among the parties concerned. We hope that all fellow member states and observer countries will establish similar organizations for the purpose of enhancing mutual understanding and traditional friendship among our peoples.

The Bishkek Declaration clarifies the stand of member states on the Syrian issue. Here I would like to reiterate that China pays close attention to the Syrian situation, supports the international community's drive for a cease-fire and peace talks, and calls on both sides of the Syrian conflict to work out a political solution to the crisis. China supports Russia's proposal that Syria surrender its chemical weapons to international control for their eventual destruction. China is ready to enhance communication and coordination with related parties through the UN Security Council, and will continue its unremitting efforts in facilitating a political settlement.

Thank you!

Work Together to Build
a 21st Century Maritime Silk Road*

October 3, 2013

China and the ASEAN countries are close neighbors sharing kinship. This year marks the 10th anniversary of the China-ASEAN strategic partnership, and our relationship is at a new historical starting point.

China places great importance on Indonesia's standing and influence in ASEAN. We wish to work with Indonesia and other ASEAN countries to ensure that China and ASEAN are good neighbors, good friends and good partners who share prosperity and security and stick together through thick and thin. Through our joint efforts, we can build a close China-ASEAN community of shared future so as to bring more benefits to both China and ASEAN and to the people in the region.

To achieve this goal, we should take the following steps:

First, build trust and good-neighborly ties. Trust is the very foundation of both interpersonal and state-to-state

---

* Part of the speech, titled "Work Together to Build a China-ASEAN Community of Shared Future", at the People's Representative Council of Indonesia.

relations. China is committed to forging a relationship with the ASEAN countries featuring sincerity, friendship, and enhanced mutual political and strategic trust.

There is no one-size-fits-all development model in the world or an unchanging development path. Both the Chinese people and the people of the ASEAN countries have embraced change and innovation with an open mind, and searched and found, in a pioneering and enterprising spirit, development paths in keeping with their specific national conditions that conform to the trend of the times. These efforts have opened up a broad prospect for their economic and social development.

We should each respect the other's right to independently choose social system and development path as well as the right to explore and pursue new ways of economic and social development, and improve its people's lives. We should have full confidence in each other's strategic choice, support each other on issues of major concern, and never deviate from the general goal of China-ASEAN strategic cooperation.

China is ready to discuss with the ASEAN countries the conclusion of a treaty of good-neighborliness, friendship and cooperation in a joint effort to build good-neighborly relations. China will continue to support ASEAN in enhancing its strength, building the ASEAN community, and playing a central role in regional cooperation.

Second, work for mutually beneficial cooperation. As a Chinese saying goes, "The interests to be considered should be the interests of all." China is ready to open its door wider to the ASEAN countries on the basis of equality and mutual benefit and enable the latter to gain more from China's development. China is prepared to upgrade the China-ASEAN Free Trade Area and increase two-way trade to US$1 trillion worth by 2020.

China is committed to enhancing its connections with the ASEAN countries. China proposes the establishment of an Asian infrastructure investment bank to support the ASEAN countries and other developing countries in our region to strengthen links in infrastructural development.

Southeast Asia has since ancient times been an important hub along the ancient Maritime Silk Road. China will strengthen maritime cooperation with the ASEAN countries, and the China-ASEAN Maritime Cooperation Fund set up by the Chinese government should be used to develop maritime partnership in a joint effort to build the Maritime Silk Road of the 21st century. China is ready to expand its practical cooperation with the ASEAN countries across the board to meet each other's needs and complement each other's strengths. This will enable us to jointly seize opportunities and meet challenges in the interest of common development and prosperity.

Third, stand together and assist each other. China and the ASEAN countries are intimate partners, and we share the responsibility for regional peace and stability. In the past, the people of China and the ASEAN countries stood together in the fight to take our destiny back into our own hands. In recent years, our peoples have stood side by side and forged strong synergy in responding to the Asian financial crisis and the international financial crisis, and in responding to the Indian Ocean tsunami and China's Wenchuan earthquake.

We should cast away the Cold War mentality, champion the new thinking of comprehensive security, common security and cooperative security, and jointly uphold peace and stability in our region. We should have deeper cooperation in disaster prevention and relief, cyber security, combating cross-border crimes, and joint law enforcement to create a more peaceful, tranquil and amicable home for the people of the region.

China is ready to work with the ASEAN countries to improve the China-ASEAN defense ministers' meeting mechanism and hold regular dialogues on regional security issues.

With regard to differences and disputes between China and some Southeast Asian countries on territorial sovereignty and maritime rights and interests, peaceful solutions should be sought, and differences and disputes should be properly handled through equality-based dialogue and friendly consultation in the overall interests of bilateral ties and regional stability.

Fourth, enhance mutual understanding and friendship. As a Chinese saying goes, "A tall tree grows from a small seedling; and the building of a nine-story tower starts with the first shovel of earth." To ensure that the tree of China-ASEAN friendship remains evergreen, the soil of social support for our relations should be fertile. Last year saw 15 million people traveling between China and the ASEAN countries, and there are over 1,000 flights between the two sides each week now. Increased interactions have nurtured a deeper bond between us and made our people feel ever-closer to each other.

We should encourage more friendly exchanges between the young people, think tanks, parliaments, NGOs and civil organizations of the two sides, which will generate further intellectual support for the growth of China-ASEAN relations and help increase the mutual understanding and friendship between our peoples. China is ready to send more volunteers to the ASEAN countries to support their development in the cultural, educational, health and medical fields. China proposes to designate 2014 as the year of China-ASEAN cultural exchanges. China will provide the ASEAN countries with 15,000 government scholarships in the coming three to five years.

Fifth, be open and inclusive. The sea is vast because it is fed by all rivers. In the long course of human history, the people of China and the ASEAN countries have created splendid and great civilizations renowned throughout the world. Ours is a diversified region where various civilizations have assimilated and interacted with one another, and this has provided an important cultural foundation for the people of China and the ASEAN countries to gain from each other's experience.

We should draw on the experience gained by other regions in development, and welcome countries outside the region to play a constructive role in promoting development and stability in the region. The outside countries, on their part, should respect the diversity of our region and do their part to facilitate its development and stability. The China-ASEAN community of shared future is closely linked with the ASEAN community and the East Asian community. The two sides need to give full rein to our respective strength to enhance diversity, harmony, inclusiveness and common progress in our region for the benefit of both our people and the people outside the region.

An increasingly cohesive China-ASEAN community of shared future conforms to the trend of the times of seeking peace, development, cooperation and mutual benefit and meets the common interests of the people of Asia and the rest of the world. This gives it a broad space and huge potential for growth.

Exchanges and Mutual Learning Make Civilizations Richer and More Colorful*

March 27, 2014

Civilizations become richer and more colorful through exchanges and mutual learning, which form an important driver for human progress and global peace and development.

To promote exchanges and mutual learning among civilizations we must adopt a correct approach with some important principles. They, in my view, contain the following:

First, civilizations come in different colors, and such diversity has made exchanges and mutual learning among civilizations relevant and valuable. Just as the sunlight has seven colors, our world is a place of dazzling colors. A civilization is the collective memory of a country or a nation. Throughout history, mankind has created and developed many colorful civilizations, from the earliest days of primitive hunting to the period of agriculture, and from booming industrial revolution to the information society. Together, they present a magnificent genetic map of the exciting march of human civilizations.

---

* Part of the speech at the UNESCO Headquarters.

"A single flower does not make spring, while one hundred flowers in full blossom bring spring to the garden." If there were only one kind of flower in the world, people would find it boring no matter how beautiful it was. Be it Chinese civilization or other civilizations in the world, they are all fruits of human progress.

I have visited the Louvre Museum in France and the Palace Museum in China, both of which house millions of art treasures. They are attractive because they present the richness of diverse civilizations. Exchanges and mutual learning among civilizations must not be built on the exclusive praise or belittling of one particular civilization. As early as over 2,000 years ago, the Chinese people came to recognize that "it is natural for things to be different." Greater exchanges and mutual learning among civilizations can further enrich the colors of various civilizations and the cultural life of people and open up still greater alternatives in the future.

Second, civilizations are equal, and such equality has made exchanges and mutual learning among civilizations possible. All human civilizations are equal in value, and they all have their respective strengths and weaknesses. No civilization is perfect on the planet. Nor is it devoid of merit. No single civilization can be judged superior to another.

I have visited many places in the world. What interested me most during the trips was to learn about differing civilizations across the five continents, what makes them different and unique, how their people think about the world and life and what they hold dear. I have visited Chichen Itza, a window on the ancient Maya civilization, and the Central Asian city of Samarkand, an icon of the ancient Islamic civilization. It is my keenly felt conviction that an attitude of equality and modesty is required if one wants to truly understand various civilizations. Taking a condescending attitude towards a civilization cannot help anyone to appreciate its essence, and may risk antagonizing it. Both history and reality show that pride and prejudice are the biggest obstacles to exchanges and mutual learning among civilizations.

Third, civilizations are inclusive, and such inclusiveness has given exchanges and mutual learning among civilizations the impetus to move forward. The ocean is vast because it refuses no rivers. All civilizations are crystallizations of mankind's diligence and wisdom. Every civilization is unique. Copying other civilizations blindly or mechanically is like cutting one's toes to fit one's shoes — impossible and highly detrimental. All achievements of civilizations deserve our respect and must be cherished.

History proves that only by interacting with and learning from others can a civilization enjoy full vitality. If all civilizations are inclusive, the so-called "clash of civilizations" can be avoided and the harmony of civilizations will become reality; as a Chinese saying goes, "Radish or cabbage, each to his own delight."

Having gone through over 5,000 years of vicissitudes, the Chinese civilization has always kept to its original root. As an icon, it contains the most profound pursuits of the Chinese nation and provides it with abundant nourishment for existence and development. Deriving from Chinese soil, it has come to its present form through constant exchanges with and learning from other civilizations.

In the 2nd century BC, China started the Silk Road leading to the Western Regions. In 138 BC and 119 BC, Envoy Zhang Qian of the Han Dynasty (206 BC-AD 220) made two trips to those regions, disseminating Chinese culture and bringing into China grapes, alfalfa, pomegranates, flax, sesame and other products.

During the Western Han Dynasty (206 BC-AD 25), China's merchant fleets sailed as far as India and Sri Lanka where they traded China's silk for colored glaze, pearls and other products.

The Tang Dynasty (618-907) saw dynamic interactions between China and other countries. Historical records reveal that China exchanged envoys with more than 70 countries, and Chang'an, the capital of Tang, bustled with envoys, merchants and students from other countries. Exchanges of such a magnitude helped spread Chinese culture to the rest of the world and introduce other cultures and products to China.

During the early 15th century, Zheng He, a famous navigator of the Ming Dynasty (1368-1644), made seven expeditions to the Western Seas, reaching many Southeast Asian countries and even Kenya on the eastern coast of Africa, leaving behind many stories of friendly exchanges between China and countries along the route.

During the late Ming and early Qing (1644-1911) dynasties, the Chinese people began to access modern science and technology through the introduction of European knowledge in the realms of astronomy, medicine, mathematics, geometry and geography, which helped broaden the horizon of Chinese people. Thereafter, exchanges and mutual learning between Chinese civilization and other civilizations became more frequent. Naturally, there were conflicts, frictions, bewilderment and denial, but the more dominant features of the period were learning, digestion, integration and innovation.

Buddhism originated in ancient India. After it was brought to China, the religion went through an extended period of integrated development with the indigenous Confucianism and Taoism, and finally became Buddhism with Chinese features, thus greatly impacting the religious beliefs, philosophy, literature, art, etiquette and customs of China. Xuan Zang, an eminent monk of the Tang Dynasty, who endured untold sufferings as he went on a pilgrimage to ancient India for Buddhist scriptures, gave full expression to the determination and fortitude of the Chinese people to learn from other cultures. I am sure you have heard of the Chinese mythological classical novel *Journey to the West* based on his stories.

The Chinese people enriched Buddhism and developed some special Buddhist thoughts in the light of Chinese culture, and helped it spread from China to Japan, Korea, Southeast Asia and beyond.

Over the last 2,000 years religions such as Buddhism,

Islam and Christianity have been introduced into China, nurturing the country's music, painting and literature. China's freehand oil painting, for instance, is an innovative combination of its own traditional painting and Western oil painting, and the works by Xu Beihong and other master painters have been widely acclaimed. China's Four Great Inventions – paper-making, gunpowder, printing and the compass, brought drastic changes to the whole world, including the European Renaissance. Its philosophy, literature, medicine, silk, porcelain and tea have been shared by the West and become part of its people's life. The book *Travels of Marco Polo* provoked widespread interest in China.

I think some of you might be familiar with the terracotta warriors and horses of the Qin Dynasty (221-207 BC), one of the eight wonders in the world. After his visit to the site, President Chirac of France remarked that a visit to Egypt would not be complete without seeing the pyramids, and that a visit to China would not be complete without seeing the terracotta warriors and horses.

In 1987 this national treasure was listed as one of UNESCO's World Cultural Heritage Sites. Many Chinese legacies are ranked as World Cultural Heritage Sites, and World Intangible Cultural Heritage Sites and are listed on the Memory of the World Register. Here, I'd like to express my heartfelt thanks to UNESCO for its contribution to the preservation and dissemination of Chinese civilization.

Today, we live in a world with different cultures, ethnic groups, skin colors, religions and social systems, and all people on the planet have become members of an intimate community of shared future.

The Chinese people have long come to appreciate the concept of "harmony without uniformity". Zuoqiu Ming, a Chinese historian who lived 2,500 years ago, recorded a few lines by Yan Zi, prime minister of the State of Qi during the Spring and Autumn Period (770-476 BC) in *Zuo's Chronicles* (*Zuo Zhuan*): "Harmony is like cooking thick soup. You need water, fire, vinegar, meat sauce, salt and plum to go with the fish or meat. It is the same with music. Only by combining the texture, length, rhythm, mood, tone, pitch and style adequately and executing them properly can you produce an excellent melody. Who can tolerate soup with nothing but water in it? Who can tolerate the same tone played again and again with one instrument?"

On the planet, there are more than 200 countries and regions inhabited by over 2,500 ethnic groups with a multitude of religions. Can we imagine a world with only one lifestyle, one language, one kind of music and one style of costume?

Victor Hugo once said that there was a prospect greater than the sea — the sky; there was a prospect greater than the sky — the human soul. Indeed, we need a mind that is broader than the sky as we approach different civilizations, which serve as water, moistening everything silently. We should encourage different civilizations to respect each other and live in harmony, so as to turn exchanges and mutual learning between civilizations into a bridge promoting friendship between peoples around the world, an engine driving human society, and a bond cementing world peace. We should draw wisdom and nourishment and seek spiritual support and psychological consolation from various civilizations, and work together to face down the challenges around the globe.

In 1987, 20 exquisite pieces of colored glaze were brought to light from an underground tomb of Famen Temple in Shaanxi, China. They proved to be Byzantine and Islamic relics brought to China during the Tang Dynasty. Marveling at these exotic relics, I was struck by the thought that we should appreciate their cultural significance rather than simply admiring their exquisiteness, and bring their inherent spirit to life instead of merely appreciating the artistic presentation of life in the past.

Build a Bridge of Friendship and Cooperation Across the Eurasian Continent[*]

April 1, 2014

China and Europe may seem far apart geographically, but we are living in the same era and on the same earth. I feel that we are as close to each other as neighbors. Both China and Europe are in a crucial stage of development, and are facing unprecedented opportunities and challenges. I hope to work with our European friends to build a bridge of friendship and cooperation across the Eurasian continent. For that we actually need to build four bridges – for the peace, growth, reform and progress of civilization – so that the China-EU comprehensive strategic partnership will take on even greater global significance.

– We need to build a bridge of peace and stability, linking the two strong forces of China and the EU. Together, China and the EU make up one tenth of the total area of the earth, and represent one fourth of the world's population. Together we hold three permanent seats on the United Nations Security Council. We all need peace, multilateralism and dialogue, instead of war, unilateralism and confrontation.

---

* Part of the speech at the College of Europe in Bruges, Belgium.

We need to enhance communication and coordination on global issues, and play a key role in safeguarding world peace and stability. Culture can spread, and so can peaceful development. China stands ready to work with the EU to let the sunlight of peace drive away the shadow of war, and the bonfire of prosperity warm up the global economy in the cold early spring, and enable all mankind to embark on the path of peaceful development and mutually beneficial cooperation.

– We need to build a bridge of growth and prosperity linking the two big markets of China and Europe. China and the EU are the two most important economies in the world, accounting for one third of the global economy. We must uphold open markets, speed up negotiations on investment agreements, proactively explore the possibility of a free trade area, and strive to achieve the ambitious goal of bringing bilateral trade to US$1 trillion-worth by 2020. We should also look to combine China-EU cooperation with the initiative of developing the Silk Road Economic Belt, so as to integrate the markets of Asia and Europe, energize the people, businesses, capital and technologies of Asia and Europe, and make China and the EU the twin engines for global economic growth.

– We need to build a bridge of reform and progress, linking the reform process in China and the EU. Both China and the EU are pursuing reforms that are unprecedented in human history, and both are sailing uncharted waters. We should enhance dialogue and cooperation on macro economy, public policy, regional development, rural development, social welfare and other fields. We need to respect each other's paths of reform, draw upon each other's reform experience, and promote world development and progress through our reform efforts.

– We need to build a bridge of common cultural prosperity linking the two major civilizations of China and Europe. China represents in an important way Eastern civilization, while Europe is the birthplace of Western civilization. The Chinese people are fond of tea, and Belgians love beer. To me, the moderate tea drinker and passionate beer lover represent two ways of understanding life and knowing the world. and I find them equally rewarding. When good friends get together, they may want to drink to their hearts' content to show their friendship. They may also choose to sit down quietly and drink tea while chatting about their lives. In China we value our ideal of "harmony without uniformity". And here in the EU people stress the need to be "united in diversity". Let us work together for all flowers of human civilization to blossom together.

In the face of all changes in the international landscape, China has always supported European integration and a bigger role in international affairs for a united, stable and prosperous EU. China will soon release its second EU policy paper to reiterate the great importance it places on the EU and on its relations with the EU. Last year, China and the EU jointly formulated the Strategic Agenda 2020 for China-EU Cooperation, setting out a host of ambitious goals in nearly a hundred fields. The two sides should work in concert to turn the blueprint into reality at an early date, and strive for greater progress in China-EU relations in the coming decade.

New Approach for Asian Security Cooperation*

May 21, 2014

Distinguished guests,

Dear colleagues,

Ladies and gentlemen,

Dear friends,

I would like to thank Foreign Minister Ahmet Davutoglu, Special Representative of the Turkish President, for his address. China has assumed the chairmanship of the Conference on Interaction and Confidence-Building Measures in Asia (CICA), so please allow me to take this opportunity to express heartfelt thanks to all sides, in particular Kazakhstan, the initiator of the CICA, and Turkey, the previous chair of the CICA, for your trust and support.

Now, let me make some observations on behalf of the People's Republic of China.

The summit today has brought together leaders and representatives from 47 countries and international organizations, including CICA member states, observers and invited

---

* Speech at the Fourth Summit of the Conference on Interaction and Confidence-Building Measures in Asia, held in Shanghai.

guests of the Shanghai Summit. Under the theme "Enhancing Dialogue, Trust and Coordination for a New Asia of Peace, Stability and Cooperation", we will discuss the important subject of security cooperation, explore policies for long-term peace and stability, and jointly promote development and prosperity. As such, this summit is of great importance to security in Asia and the world at large, and will have far-reaching consequences.

Asia today is home to 67 percent of the world's population, and accounts for one third of the global economy. It is a place where diverse civilizations and nations meet and interact. Peace and development in Asia are closely connected with the future of mankind, and Asia's stability and revival are a blessing to the peace and development of the rest of the world.

Asia today, though facing risks and challenges, is still the most dynamic and promising region in the world. Peace, development and mutually beneficial cooperation are the main trend in the region, and countries in the region generally prefer policies that address differences and disputes through consultation and negotiation. Asia enjoys a rising status in the international strategic landscape, and plays an increasingly important role in promoting a multi-polar world and democracy in international relations. Such a healthy situation in the region has not come easily and ought to be doubly cherished.

Asia today is engaged in vibrant cooperation in the economic field. Cooperation in the security field is making progress despite difficulties, and various cooperation mechanisms are becoming more dynamic. Asia has come to a crucial stage in security cooperation at which we need to build on past achievements and strive for new progress.

As a Chinese saying goes, "A wise man changes his way as circumstances change; a knowledgeable person alters his means as times evolve." We need to keep pace with changing circumstances and evolving times. One cannot live in the 21st century with the outdated thinking of the era of the Cold War and zero-sum game. We believe that it is necessary to advocate common, comprehensive, cooperative and sustainable security in Asia. We need to innovate our security concept, establish a new regional security cooperation architecture, and jointly build a road towards security in Asia that is shared by and of benefit to all.

Common security means respecting and ensuring the security of each and every country. Asia is a region of great diversity. The countries there differ in size, wealth and strength. They vary in historical and cultural traditions as well as social systems, and have different security interests and aspirations. However, we are all part of the same Asian family. With our interests and security so closely intertwined, we will sink or swim together, and we are increasingly becoming a community of shared future.

Security must be universal. We cannot have the security of just one or a few countries while leaving the rest insecure, in no way can we accept the so-called absolute security of one at the expense of the security of others. Otherwise, just as a Kazakh proverb aptly puts it, "One who tries to blow out another's oil lamp will get his beard singed."

Security must be equal. Every country has the equal right to participate in the security affairs of the region as well as the responsibility for upholding regional security. No country should attempt to dominate regional security affairs or infringe upon the legitimate rights and interests of other countries.

Security must be inclusive. We should turn Asia's diversity and the differences among Asian countries into a vital driving force for regional security cooperation. We should abide by the basic norms governing international relations such as respecting sovereignty, independence and territorial integrity and non-interference in internal affairs, respect the social systems and development paths chosen by individual countries, and fully respect and accommodate the legitimate security concerns of all parties. To buttress and entrench a military alliance targeted at a third party is not conducive to common security.

Comprehensive security means upholding security in both traditional and non-traditional fields. Asia's security challenges are extremely complicated, and include a range of flashpoints and sensitive issues, as well as ethnic and religious problems. The challenges brought by terrorism, transnational crime, environmental safety, cyber security, energy security, and major natural disasters are clearly on the rise. Traditional and non-traditional security threats are interwoven. Security is a growing issue in both scope and implication.

We should take full account of the historical background and reality of Asia's security issues, adopt a multi-pronged and holistic approach, and enhance regional security governance in a coordinated way. While tackling the immediate security challenges facing the region we should also make plans for addressing potential security threats, and avoid a fragmented and palliative approach that only treats the symptoms.

We should have zero tolerance for terrorism, separatism and extremism, strengthen international and regional cooperation, and step up the fight against these three forces, so as to bring peace and happiness to the people of this region.

Cooperative security means promoting the security of both individual countries and the region as a whole through dialogue and cooperation. As the proverb goes, "Strength does not come from the muscles in the arms, but from the unison of the heart." We should engage in sincere and in-depth dialogue and communication to increase strategic mutual trust, reduce mutual misgivings, seek common ground while resolving differences, and live in harmony with each other. We should bear in mind the common security interests of all countries, and start with low-sensitivity areas to build the awareness of meeting security challenges through cooperation. We should expand the scope and means of cooperation and promote peace and security through cooperation. We should stay committed to resolving disputes through peaceful means, stand against the arbitrary use or threat of force, oppose the provocation and escalation of tensions for self-interest, and eschew the practice of shifting trouble onto neighbors and seeking gain at the expense of others.

In the final analysis, let the people of Asia run the affairs of Asia, solve the problems of Asia and uphold the security of Asia. The people of Asia have the capability and wisdom to achieve peace and stability in the region through enhanced cooperation.

Asia is open to the world. While enhancing our own cooperation with each other, countries in Asia must also firmly commit ourselves to cooperation with countries in other continents, other regions and international organizations. We welcome all parties to play a positive and constructive role in promoting Asia's security and cooperation, and work together to achieve mutually beneficial outcomes for all.

Sustainable security means that we need to focus on both development and security, so that security will be durable. As a Chinese saying goes, "For a tree to grow tall, a strong and solid root is essential; for a river to reach far, an unimpeded source is necessary." Development is the foundation of security, and security the precondition for development. The tree of peace does not grow on barren land, and the fruits of development are not harvested amidst the flames of war. For most Asian countries, development means the greatest security and the master key to regional security issues.

To build an Asian security stronghold that can stand the test of any gale we need to focus on development, zealously improve people's lives and narrow the wealth gap so as to cement the foundation of security. We need to advance the process of common development and regional integration, foster sound interaction between regional economic cooperation and security cooperation for synchronized progress, and promote sustainable security through sustainable development.

Ladies and gentlemen,

Dear friends,

The CICA is the largest and most representative regional security forum with the largest number of participants. Over the past two decades the CICA has undertaken the responsibility to strengthen mutual trust and coordination and promote Asia's security and stability. It has followed the principle of consensus through consultation and made an important contribution to increasing understanding, seeking common ground and expanding cooperation.

Today more than ever, the Asian people wish for peace and stability, and the need to work together to tackle challenges to security is greater than before.

China proposes that we make the CICA a security dialogue and cooperation platform that covers the whole of Asia and, on that basis, explore the establishment of a regional security cooperation architecture. China believes that it is advisable to increase the frequency of the CICA foreign ministers' meetings and possibly summits as circumstances change, so as to strengthen the political guidance of the CICA and chart a blueprint for its development.

China proposes that we enhance the capacity and the institutions of the CICA, support improving the functions of the CICA secretariat, establish a defense consultation mechanism of member states and a task force for supervising the implementation of confidence-building measures in various areas within the CICA framework, and enhance exchanges and cooperation in counter-terrorism, business, tourism, environmental protection, and cultural and people-to-people exchanges.

China proposes that we put in place a nongovernmental exchange network for various parties through holding CICA nongovernmental forums and other means, so as to lay a solid social foundation for spreading the CICA concept of security, increasing the CICA's influence and promoting regional security governance.

China proposes that we strengthen the inclusiveness and openness of the CICA. We need to step up coordination and cooperation with other relevant organizations in the region, and expand dialogue and communication with other regions and relevant international organizations.

China will fulfill its responsibilities as CICA chairman and work with other parties to further improve the status and role of the CICA so that together we can raise security cooperation to a higher level.

Ladies and gentlemen,

Dear friends,

China is a staunch force for upholding peace in the region and the world as a whole and for promoting common development. The Five Principles of Peaceful Coexistence initiated by China together with India and Myanmar have become basic norms governing state-to-state relations. China remains committed to seeking the peaceful settlement of disputes with other countries over territorial sovereignty and maritime rights and interests. China has completely resolved, through friendly consultations, land boundary issues with 12 of its 14 neighboring countries. As an active participant in regional security cooperation, China, jointly with other relevant countries, initiated the Shanghai Cooperation Organization and proposed the concept of mutual trust, mutual benefit, equality and coordination. China supports ASEAN, the SAARC and the LAS in playing a positive role in regional affairs. China and Russia jointly proposed an Asia-Pacific security and cooperation initiative, which has played an important role in strengthening and maintaining peace and stability in the Asia-Pacific region. China works to push forward the Six-Party Talks Concerning the Korean Peninsula, and supports peace and reconstruction in Afghanistan, making unremitting efforts in solving international and regional flashpoint issues through dialogue and negotiation. China joined forces with countries in the region and the wider international community to tackle the Asian financial crisis and the international financial crisis, making its due contribution to promoting regional and global economic growth.

China is firmly committed to the path of peaceful development and the mutually beneficial strategy of opening up. It seeks to develop friendly relations and cooperation with other countries on the basis of the Five Principles of Peaceful Coexistence. China's peaceful development begins here in

Asia, finds its support in Asia and delivers tangible benefits to Asia.

"Neighbors wish each other well, just as family members do." China always pursues friendship and partnership with its neighbors, seeks to bring amity, security and common prosperity, and works hard to ensure that its development brings benefits to all other countries in Asia. China will work with other countries to speed up the development of a Silk Road Economic Belt and a 21st Century Maritime Silk Road, and hopes that the Asian Infrastructure Investment Bank can be launched at an early date. China will be more involved in the regional cooperation process, and play its part to ensure that development and security in Asia facilitate each other and are mutually reinforcing.

As the saying goes, "Readiness to converge with others makes a mountain high and a river mighty." As a strong champion of the Asian security concept, China also works to put such a security concept into practice. China will take solid steps to strengthen security dialogues and cooperation with other parties, and jointly explore the formulation of a code of conduct for regional security and an Asian security partnership program, making Asian countries good partners who trust one another and cooperate on an equal footing.

China is ready to introduce mechanisms for regular exchange and cooperation with countries in the region to jointly combat the three forces of terrorism, separatism and extremism. China is ready to discuss with other countries in the region the creation of an Asian forum for security cooperation in law enforcement and an Asian security emergency response center, to enhance security cooperation in law enforcement and better respond to major security emergencies. China calls for exchanges and mutual learning among different civilizations and religions through various means, such as conferences for dialogues among Asian civilizations, so that we will be able to draw on each other's experiences and achieve common progress.

Ladies and gentlemen,

Dear friends,

The Chinese people, in their pursuit of the Chinese Dream of great national renewal, stand ready to support and help all other peoples in Asia to realize their own great dreams. Let us work together to realize the Asian dream of lasting peace and common development, and make a greater contribution to advancing the noble cause of peace and development of mankind.

Thank you!

Promote the Silk Road Spirit,
Strengthen Sino-Arab Cooperation*

June 5, 2014

Your Excellency Prime Minister Jaber,
Secretary-General El Araby of the League of Arab States,
Heads of delegations,
Ladies and gentlemen,
Dear friends,

Al Salam aleikum![1] Good morning! I am very happy to-day to get together with our Arab friends and discuss the development of the China-Arab States Cooperation Forum (CASCF) and Sino-Arab relations. Let me begin by extending, on behalf of the Chinese government and our people and in my own name, a warm welcome to all the guests, and let me offer my hearty congratulations on the convening of the sixth ministerial conference of the CASCF!

Arab friends always feel like old friends to me. This is attributable both to the warm and sincere attitude with which we treat each other, and to the long history of exchanges between the Chinese and Arab peoples.

---

* Speech at the opening ceremony of the Sixth Ministerial Conference of the China-Arab States Cooperation Forum in Beijing.

Looking back on the history of exchanges between the Chinese and Arab peoples, we immediately think of the land Silk Road and the maritime spice route. Our ancestors "crossed the desert for months on end on post-horses", and "sailed the oceans day and night", putting themselves at the forefront of friendly exchanges between different nations in the ancient world. Gan Ying, Zheng He, and Ibn Battuta were goodwill envoys for Sino-Arab exchanges whom we still remember today. It was by way of the Silk Road that China's four great inventions – paper-making, gunpowder, printing, and the compass – were transmitted via the Arab region to Europe, and it was also by way of the Silk Road that the Arabs' astronomy, calendrical system, and medicines were introduced to China, marking an important chapter in the history of exchanges and mutual learning between civilizations.

For hundreds of years the spirit embodied by the Silk Road, namely peace and cooperation, openness and inclusiveness, mutual learning, and mutual benefit, has passed down through the generations. The Chinese and Arab peoples have supported each other in maintaining national dignity and safeguarding state sovereignty, helped each other in exploring development and achieving national rejuvenation, and learned from each other in encouraging people-to-people and cultural exchanges and revitalizing national culture.

We will not forget the promise to support the cause of the Palestinian people that China made to the Arab states – with which we had not yet established diplomatic relations – at the Bandung Conference 60 years ago. Nor will we forget the votes cast over 40 years ago by 13 Arab states, together with our African friends, for the People's Republic of China (PRC) to regain its UN seat. We will not forget the 10,000 Chinese doctors who worked to save lives in the Arab states. Nor will we forget the most generous aid China received from our Arab brothers after the massive Wenchuan earthquake.

Ladies and gentlemen,

Dear friends,

The next decade will be a crucial period for the development of both China and the Arab states. China has entered a decisive phase in its drive to complete the building of a moderately prosperous society in all respects, and the fulfillment of this goal represents a crucial step towards the Chinese Dream of national rejuvenation. To do so, we have made overall plans for driving our reform to a deeper level. A key focus of this drive is to develop all-round international cooperation within an open economic system of quality and vitality, and to expand our common interests with various countries and regions in pursuit of mutual benefit. The Middle East is in a phase of unprecedented change, and the Arab states are making efforts to seek reform in their own way. The challenge of achieving national renewal calls on us to carry forward the Silk Road spirit, bolster development and cooperation, and constantly reinforce a strategic Sino-Arab relationship of comprehensive cooperation and common development.

To promote the Silk Road spirit, we need to boost mutual learning between civilizations. There is no such thing as a good or a bad civilization. Rather, different civilizations are enriched through exchange. As a Chinese philosopher said, "The matching of different colors leads to greater beauty, and the combination of different musical instruments creates harmony and peace." China and the Arab states have always viewed each other with an open and inclusive attitude, and engaged in dialogues and exchanges rather than conflict and confrontation. We have set a good example of harmonious coexistence between countries with different social systems, beliefs, and cultural traditions. China will never falter in its support for the Arab states in safeguarding their national cultural traditions, and will oppose all discrimination and prejudice against any ethnic groups and religions. We should work together to advocate tolerance towards different civilizations, and prevent extremist forces and ideas from creating division between us.

To promote the Silk Road spirit, we need to respect each other's choice of development path. "People don't need to wear the same shoes; they should find what suit their feet. Governments don't have to adopt the same model of governance; they should find what benefits their people." Whether the path of a country is the right one is a matter to be decided by its people. Just as we do not expect all flowers to be violets, we cannot demand that countries with diverse cultural traditions, historical experiences, and contemporary national conditions should adopt the same development mode. That would make for a dull world. The Arab states are making their own efforts to explore their own development paths. We are willing to share our experience of governance with our Arab friends, so that each can draw on the wisdom of the other's time-honored civilization and development mode.

To promote the Silk Road spirit, we need to focus on mutually beneficial cooperation. What China pursues is common development, which means we are aiming for a better life for the Chinese people and for the peoples of other countries. In the next five years, China's imports will surpass US$10 trillion-worth, and our outward foreign direct investment (FDI) will surpass US$500 billion. In 2013, China's imports from the Arab states were worth US$140 billion, accounting for only 7 percent of the annual US$2 trillion in imported goods that China plans for the years ahead; and China's outward FDI to the Arab states was US$2.2 billion, accounting for only 2.2 percent of the US$100 billion in annual outward FDI that China plans for the years ahead. These facts represent an indicator of great potential and opportunity. China is happy to connect its own development with the development of the Arab states, and to support them in promoting employment, industrialization and economic growth.

To promote the Silk Road spirit, we need to advocate dialogue and peace. China firmly supports the Middle East peace process and the establishment of an independent State of Palestine, with full sovereignty, based on the 1967 borders, and with East Jerusalem as its capital. We hope the parties involved will take concrete measures to remove obstacles to peace talks and break the stalemate as soon as possible.

China respects the reasonable demands of the Syrian people, and supports the early adoption of the Geneva communiqué and the opening of an inclusive political transition, to bring about a political resolution to the Syrian issue. China is deeply concerned about the humanitarian situation in Syria, and will provide a new batch of humanitarian aid to Syrian refugees in Jordan and Lebanon to alleviate their plight. China supports the establishment of a Middle East nuclear-weapon-free zone, and opposes any attempt to change the political landscape of the Middle East. China will play a constructive role in regional affairs, speak up for justice, and work with the Arab states to encourage dialogue as a way to find the greatest common denominator on issues of concern to all parties. We will direct a greater level of diplomatic effort to the proper settlement of regional flashpoints.

Ladies and gentlemen,

Dear friends,

The Belt and Road, namely the Silk Road Economic Belt and the Maritime Silk Road of the 21st Century, represent paths towards mutual benefit which will bring about closer economic integration among the countries involved, promote development of their infrastructure and institutional innovation, create new economic and employment growth areas, and enhance their capacity to achieve endogenous growth and to protect themselves against risks.

As friends brought together by the Silk Road, China and the Arab states are natural partners in a joint effort to develop the Belt and Road.

To develop the Belt and Road, the two sides need to follow the principles of extensive consultation, joint contribution, and shared benefits. "Extensive consultation" requires that we pool collective wisdom and carry out relevant initiatives through negotiations, so that the interests and concerns of both sides are balanced, and the wisdom and ideas of both sides are reflected. "Joint contribution" requires that we give full play to the strengths and potential of both sides, so that a combination of efforts will lead to sustained progress. As the saying goes, "A tower can be built one stone at a time; a pool can be formed from single drops of water." So we must persist in doing so. "Shared benefits" requires that both peoples benefit equally from the fruits of development, with a view to joining China and the Arab states even more closely through our shared interests and destiny.

To develop the Belt and Road, the two sides need to be both far-sighted and down-to-earth. To be far-sighted, we need to produce the optimum top-level design, identify our orientation and goals, and establish a "1+2+3" cooperation pattern.

"1" refers to cooperation in energy as the core. We will strengthen cooperation in the whole industrial chain of oil and natural gas, safeguard the security of energy transport corridors, and establish mutually beneficial, safe and reliable strategic cooperation in energy based on long-term friendship.

"2" refers to "two wings" – one being infrastructure and the other being trade and investment. We will strengthen cooperation on major development programs and landmark projects for public wellbeing, and devise relevant institutional mechanisms to facilitate bilateral trade and investment. China will encourage its enterprises to import more non-oil products from the Arab states and optimize its trade structure, in a bid to increase the bilateral trade volume from last year's US$240 billion-worth to US$600 billion-worth in the decade ahead. China will also encourage its enterprises to invest in energy, petrochemicals, agriculture, manufacturing, and services in the Arab states, aiming to increase China's investment in the non-financial sector in the Arab states from last year's US$10 billion to over US$60 billion in the following decade.

"3" refers to using three advanced technologies – nuclear energy, space satellites and new energy – as breakthrough levers in an effort to raise the level of pragmatic Sino-Arab cooperation. The two sides may discuss the establishment of technology transfer centers, jointly develop training centers in the Arab states for the peaceful use of nuclear energy, and launch programs to introduce China's BeiDou Navigation Satellite System to the Arab states.

To be down-to-earth, we need to aim for quick successes. As an Arab proverb goes, "Words proved by action are the most powerful." We need to step up negotiations on programs on which consensus has already been reached and for which the foundations have been laid – programs such as the Free Trade Area between China and the Cooperation Council for the Arab States of the Gulf, the China-United

Arab Emirates Joint Investment Fund, and the Arab states' participation in the preparations for the Asian Infrastructure Investment Bank. These programs must be launched as soon as the conditions are ripe. The sooner we have substantial results to show from the development of the Belt and Road Initiative, the easier it will be to keep the various parties motivated and set examples for other programs.

The two sides need to rely on and enhance the traditional friendship between China and the Arab states. The fostering of friendship between the peoples of the two sides represents a key foundation and an important element of the Belt and Road Initiative. I hereby declare that China and the Arab states have decided to designate 2014 and 2015 as Years of Sino-Arab Friendship and to hold a series of friendly exchange events. We are also willing to enhance cultural exchanges by hosting arts festivals, to encourage more students to engage in social exchanges with the other side such as study, and to strengthen cooperation in tourism, aviation, journalism, and publishing. In the next three years China will train another 6,000 Arab people in various skills to be applied in the Arab states. We will share our experiences of development and poverty alleviation with the Arab states, and introduce those of our advanced technologies that are suited to their needs. In the next decade, China will organize mutual visits and exchanges by 10,000 Chinese and Arab artists, promote and support dedicated cooperation between 200 Chinese and Arab cultural institutions, and invite and support 500 Arab cultural and artistic personages to study in China.

Ladies and gentlemen,

Dear friends,

The establishment of the CASCF was a strategic step taken for the long-term development of Sino-Arab relations. After 10 years, the Forum has become an effective means by which we are able to enrich the strategic content of Sino-Arab relations and promote pragmatic cooperation between the two sides. Our joint efforts to develop the Belt and Road Initiative represent a new opportunity and a new starting point for upgrading the Forum. Only by seizing this opportunity will we be able to maintain our current progress while ensuring sustainable development in the future; and only by starting from this new point will we be able to broaden our prospects and give further impetus to development. In one sentence, the Forum needs to serve as the basis of and support for further development between the two sides.

We should take the Forum as a lever to enhance communication on policy. Instead of sidestepping the differences and problems between us, we need to treat each other in a frank and honest way, communicate with each other with regard to our respective foreign policies and development strategies, enhance political trust, and facilitate coordination strategies, with a view to providing policy support for our cooperation.

We should take the Forum as a lever to extend cooperation in a pragmatic fashion. The development initiatives of both sides are mutually complementary. We need to promote the sharing of resources on both sides, and talk and cooperate with each other with the greatest possible frankness and sincerity. Instead of trying to achieve headline-grabbing successes, collective cooperation should aim for measures that lay the foundations for long-term development.

We should take the Forum as a lever to forge ahead with innovation. Innovation constitutes the lifeblood of the Forum. The two sides need to adopt new ideas, new measures, and new mechanisms in a bid to resolve the difficulties that we encounter in pragmatic cooperation, and clear practical bottlenecks and unlock potential for cooperation through a spirit of reform and innovation.

Ladies and gentlemen,

Dear friends,

The rapid development of Sino-Arab relations has created a close link in the future of the peoples of both sides. In Zhejiang Province where I used to work, there is a Jordanian businessman named Muhamad who runs a genuine Arabian restaurant in Yiwu City, where a lot of Arab business people gather. Through bringing genuine Arabian cuisine to Yiwu, he has achieved business success in this prosperous Chinese city, and has gone on to marry a Chinese girl and settle down in China. Integrating his own goals with the Chinese dream of happiness, this young Arab man has built a marvelous life for himself through his perseverance – he embodies a perfect combination of the Chinese Dream and the Arab Dream.

Both the Chinese and the Arab nations have created splendid civilizations, and both have experienced setbacks amidst the changing times of modern history. Therefore, national rejuvenation has become the goal of both sides. Let us work shoulder to shoulder to promote the Silk Road spirit, strengthen Sino-Arab cooperation, realize the Chinese Dream and Arab revitalization, and strive for the lofty cause of peace and development for humankind!

Shukran![2] Thank you!

Notes

[1] *Al Salam aleikum*, Arabic, meaning "Hello".

[2] *Shukran*, Arabic, meaning "Thank you".

Strive for Economic Development with South Asian Countries Through the Belt and Road[*]

September 18, 2014

China has always been a peace-loving nation. The pursuit of peace, amity and harmony is an integral part of the Chinese character. China has always believed that "the strong should not oppress the weak and the rich should not abuse the poor". Even in ancient times, China had come to the conclusion that "a warlike state, however big it may be, will eventually perish". "Peace is of paramount importance", "seeking harmony without uniformity", "replacing weapons of war with jade and silk", and "achieving universal peace" – axioms like these have been passed down in China from generation to generation. Historically, China was long a great power, but it brought to the world ideas such as peace and products such as silk, tea and porcelain. The Chinese concepts of "universal peace" and "universal love" and the Indian concepts of *Vasudhaiva Kutumbakam* (the world being one family) and *Ahimsa* (non-violence) are very much alike.

---

* Part of the speech, titled "In Joint Pursuit of a Dream of National Renewal", at the Indian Council of World Affairs.

Both China and India consider harmony as the way towards a better future for the world and hope that all countries will live in harmony and peace.

The Chinese nation has always valued learning, as evidenced by well-known Chinese sayings such as "Only by learning extensively and accumulating profound knowledge can one be ready to achieve something," "When walking in the company of two other men, there are bound to be things I can learn from them. I will absorb the good qualities and avoid the shortcomings," and "One needs to study what is good, constantly inquire about it, carefully reflect on it, clearly distinguish it and earnestly practice it." It is this spirit of learning, characterized by humility and inclusiveness that has enabled China to make continuous progress for thousands of years. I have often emphasized that our goal is to be a great learning nation. We must avoid complacency and self-importance. Instead, we must be modest and humble, study hard and continue to enhance our capabilities.

China has always valued good neighborliness. Keeping its word, and promoting harmony among all nations, have always been the guiding principles of China's foreign policy. China sees its neighborhood as the key to its wellbeing and the foundation of its development and prosperity. We have proposed the principles of amity, sincerity, mutual benefit and inclusiveness as guidelines for our neighborhood diplomacy. The very purpose is to express our genuine desire to live in harmony with our neighbors and concentrate on common development. We want to work together with our neighbors and expand the results of cooperation, so that we can all share the fruits of development.

China, a country with over 1.3 billion people, has managed in just a few decades to complete a journey of development that took developed countries several centuries. This is a historic achievement. That said, we are also soberly aware of the fact that China remains the biggest developing country in the world and is still at the primary stage of socialism. It is true that its economic aggregate is substantial, but when divided by 1.3 billion people, its per capita GDP only ranks around 80th in the world. It will be a long and arduous task to ensure that we can all lead a better life.

For quite some time to come China will focus on economic development, and on this basis will work to promote social progress across the board. China has set a development goal for itself: to double 2010 GDP and per capita urban and rural incomes, and complete the building of a moderately prosperous society in all respects by 2020, and to build China into a modern socialist country that is prosperous, democratic, culturally advanced and harmonious by the middle of this century. We have identified this goal as the Chinese Dream of national rejuvenation.

To realize the Chinese Dream, China needs a long-term peaceful and stable external environment. Only the path of peaceful development can lead China to its development goal. After suffering from the pain of over 100 years of incessant warfare in modern times, the Chinese people do not want to see such a tragic experience repeated anywhere in the world. As the ancient Chinese philosophy teaches us, "Do not do unto others what you do not want others to do unto you." China cherishes and loves peace. And it is firm in its resolve to maintain peace.

The peoples of South Asia, from Nepal to Maldives, and from Afghanistan to Bangladesh, have yearned for a better life and pursued national revitalization. All this promises a bright future for South Asia. I am convinced that South Asia, a subcontinent that holds infinite promise and potential, will become a new pole of growth in Asia and beyond.

A South Asia that enjoys peace, stability, development and prosperity serves the interests of the countries and people in the region and of China as well. China wants to live in harmony with all countries in the region and contribute its share to the development of the region. The Belt and Road Initiative that China has proposed is precisely aimed at strengthening connectivity among countries along the routes of the traditional land and maritime Silk Roads, with a view to achieving common prosperity, complementarity in trade, and closer people-to-people ties. China hopes that, propelled by the two "wings" of the Belt and the Road, its economy will take off together with those of South Asian countries.

China and the countries of South Asia are important partners in cooperation. Our cooperation, like a massive treasure long awaiting discovery, offers us great prospects. In the next five years, China will work with South Asian countries to increase bilateral trade to US$150 billion and its investment in South Asia to US$30 billion, and provide US$20 billion in concessional loans to the region. China will expand people-to-people and cultural exchanges with South Asia. We plan to offer 10,000 scholarships, training opportunities for 5,000 people, and exchange and training programs for 5,000 youth, and train 5,000 Chinese language teachers for South Asia in the next five years. China will work with the countries of South Asia to implement the China-South Asia Partnership Initiative for Science and Technology, give full play to the role of China-South Asia Expo, and build new platforms for mutually beneficial cooperation.

China is the biggest neighbor of South Asia and India is the largest country in South Asia. China is ready to work together with India and make a greater contribution to the development of the region, so that the three billion people living on the two sides of the Himalayas can enjoy peace, friendship, stability and prosperity.

Accelerate the Building of the Belt and Road*

November 4, 2014

The initiative of the Silk Road Economic Belt and the 21st Century Maritime Silk Road is a response to the demands of the times and the desire of countries to accelerate their development. It provides a huge inclusive platform for development. With deep historical roots and cultural foundations, it can combine the fast-growing Chinese economy with the interests of countries along the Belt and Road. We need to concentrate on this initiative. Our diplomacy with neighboring countries is characterized by amity, sincerity, mutual benefit and inclusiveness, and keeping friendly relations with countries, both close and distant, in the hope of winning recognition, friendship and support from countries along the routes.

The Belt and the Road run through the Eurasian continent, connecting the Asia-Pacific economic community in the east and entering the European economic community in the west. China and many countries along the routes share common interests, such as boosting the economy, improving

---

* Main points of the speech at the eighth meeting of the Leading Group for Financial and Economic Affairs under the CPC Central Committee.

standards of living, tackling crises, and accelerating economic adjustment. Historically, the land Silk Road and the maritime Silk Road were major corridors for economic and cultural exchanges between China and Central Asia, Southeast Asia, South Asia, West Asia, East Africa, and Europe. The initiative has won wide recognition as it renews and promotes the ancient Silk Road.

This initiative can help expand and advance opening up to a higher level. After more than 30 years of reform and opening up, the Chinese economy is in a new phase, shifting the focus from "bringing in" to a balance between "bringing in" and "going global". The market, energy, and investment have been deeply integrated with the rest of the world. Only by opening up and further integrating into the global economy, can China achieve sustainable development.

To accelerate the building of the Belt and Road, we should be sincere with countries along the routes, true in word and resolute in deed. We will cooperate with other countries involved on the principle of mutual benefit so that they will gain from China's development. We will implement inclusive development so that all the countries share opportunities, meet challenges together, and work for common prosperity. We should design an overall strategy for the initiative, prepare timetables and road maps for the coming years as soon as possible, and identify areas of opportunity ripe for an early harvest. We should focus on implementation of projects progressing from the easier to the more difficult, from the near to the distant, working from a point to a line and then to an area. We will build solid economic and trade cooperation, and implement key projects step by step in a down-to-earth manner.

To accelerate the building of the Belt and Road, we should focus on key landmark projects and strive to extract positive results as early as possible. We will help countries along the routes to carry out planning of national or inter-regional infrastructure projects involving transport, electricity, telecommunications and others, jointly promote early stage pre-research, and propose a list of projects for the good of bilateral or multilateral interests. We will attach great importance to and launch a number of projects that can help improve standards of living in the countries involved. We should advance economic cooperation and, at the same time, boost educational, tourist, academic, artistic and other people-to-people exchanges between China and these countries to a new level.

The Belt and Road Initiative is a long-term program, and it needs to be properly coordinated. We need to strike a proper balance between the role of government and that of the market, so that the market mechanism can be effective. We encourage state-owned enterprises, private enterprises and other enterprises to participate in the initiative, while giving full play to the government's role. We should direct our attention to building the mechanism and platform for inter-state and inter-regional economic and trade cooperation, develop investment and trade models in line with local conditions, and thus advance the work under institutional arrangements.

We will provide more foreign aid, employ the unique strengths of development-oriented finance and policy-based finance, and actively guide private capital to participate in the building of the Belt and Road. We should coordinate the relations between departments and regions, which should both strengthen the division of labor and work in concert.

We will use innovative thinking in running the Asian Infrastructure Investment Bank (AIIB) and the Silk Road Fund. The AIIB was initiated by China and set up with other countries to finance infrastructure construction in the countries along the Belt and Road, and to promote economic cooperation. The Fund was established to provide direct support to the Belt and Road construction with our financial strength. We should work in accordance with international conventions, take as reference theories and long-term practical experience that existing multilateral financial institutions have accumulated, make and follow strict rules and regulations, improve transparency and inclusiveness, and identify and start the first batch of projects. The AIIB and the Silk Road Fund are complementary to existing global and regional development banks rather than any kind of substitute. They will work under the current international economic and financial order.

Connectivity Spearheads Development and Partnership Enables Cooperation[*]

November 8, 2014

Your Excellency President Abdul Hamid,
Your Excellency President Choummaly Sayasone,
Your Excellency President Tsakhiagiin Elbegdorj,
Your Excellency President U Thein Sein,
Your Excellency President Emomali Rahmon,
Your Excellency Prime Minister Samdech Hun Sen,
Your Excellency Prime Minister Nawaz Sharif,
Ladies and gentlemen,
Dear friends,

Let me begin by thanking all of you for coming to Beijing for this Dialogue on Strengthening Connectivity Partnership. It is a vivid testimony to the deep friendship and cooperation existing in our relations and an expression of the support from you that we consider so important to China's hosting of the 22nd APEC Economic Leaders' Meeting.

"Friends and neighbors become closer when they visit each other more often." Meeting face-to-face and exchanging

---

* Speech at the Dialogue on Strengthening Connectivity Partnership in Beijing.

views among neighboring countries on major issues is ever more necessary. China, as the host of the 22nd APEC Economic Leaders' Meeting, has made Asia-Pacific connectivity one of the topics of the meeting. Given the importance of the issue and the fact that many Asian countries and international organizations are interested and eager to get involved in the discussions, we have decided to have this meeting after consulting with stakeholders so that we can discuss together how we can best advance development in Asia.

You might have heard of a Chinese fable describing the old man who tried to move two mountains. Thousands of years ago, there was an elderly named Yu Gong, meaning Foolish Old Man, who lived in a remote village surrounded by high mountains. He resolved to remove the two mountains obstructing his access to the outside world. Relatives and neighbors all cautioned him against the idea, but Yu Gong was undeterred and continued with the job with his children and grandchildren day in and day out. He said that the mountains would not grow any bigger or taller but humans would grow from generation to generation. So long as they persevered, there would be a day when the mountains were removed. Yu Gong's perseverance moved the Heavenly God. Through the joint efforts of man and God, the mountains were removed and Yu Gong's village was connected with the outside world.

Humanity has yearned to connect since ancient times. Our ancestors braved extremely harsh conditions to create opportunities to connect. The Silk Road was just a case in point, giving the Asian peoples the well-deserved title of pioneers in this field.

As humanity moves forward, our society is progressing. At present, with the impact of the international financial crisis lingering, global economic growth and trade have both slowed down. At the same time, a new round of industrial and technological revolution is in the making, free trade arrangements at regional level are mushrooming, and structural adjustment, reform and innovation are becoming a prevailing trend of the world. Against such a backdrop, Asian countries, built on their traditional strengths in resources, manufacturing capacity, and savings, and as the world's workshop, ought to redouble their efforts and join hands to build Asian value, innovation, investment and markets, with a view to cultivating new growth areas and new competitive edges. In achieving all these goals, connectivity holds the key.

The connectivity we talk about today is not merely about building roads and bridges or making linear connections between different surface places. More importantly, it should be a three-way combination of infrastructure, institutions and people-to-people exchanges, and a five-way process of policy communication, infrastructure connectivity, trade links, capital flows, and understanding among peoples. It is a wide-ranging, multi-dimensional, vibrant and open connectivity network that pools talent and resources from all stakeholders.

Asia faces both opportunities and difficulties in developing connectivity. The challenges come from diversity of systems

and laws in various countries, the divergent needs and requirements among stakeholders, and the less than satisfacto-
ry coordination between existing mechanisms. The issue of
funding stands out as the most challenging. According to the
Asian Development Bank estimate, Asia as a whole needs as
much as US$730 billion per year in infrastructure investment
between now and 2020. To address this and other problems,
efforts on the part of a single or even several countries are
far from adequate. Only by building extensive partnerships
where all will think and work in unison, can we expect to
achieve positive results.

— We need to achieve coordinated development among
Asian countries. Asian countries attach great importance to
connectivity and many of them have worked out national
plans for infrastructure development. It is time for us to integrate such strategies and plans, identify the priority areas
and projects, and pool together our resources to make coordinated progress in implementation. This will help bring
down the cost of logistics, create demand and employment,
pool our comparative and latecomer advantages, secure favorable positions in the global supply chain, industrial chain
and value chain, raise our comprehensive competitiveness,
and bring about a new situation in Asian development characterized by robust, sustainable and balanced growth. Asian
countries are like a cluster of bright lanterns. Only when
they are linked together, can they light up the night sky of
our continent.

— We need to build a more open economy in Asia. Facing

the current trends towards multipolarity, economic globalization, cultural diversity and increased use of IT, no country can expect to develop on its own behind closed doors. Seclusion will lead nowhere. A country can only develop by staying open to the outside world. Asian countries should follow open regionalism, refrain from forming exclusive blocs or targeting third countries, and urge countries both within and outside of the region to make the best of their capabilities, complement each other's strengths, and share their gains. Countries sharing common borders need to be more open to each other, through measures such as negotiating and signing transport, trade, and investment agreements, connecting their cross-border infrastructure, and coordinating and aligning their regulations in various areas.

It is imperative to resolve through consultation issues that affect connectivity such as institutions, policies and standards, so as to reduce the costs and time required for cross-border flows of people, goods and capital. We need to carry out cooperation in mutual information sharing, mutual recognition of scrutiny, and mutual law-enforcement assistance in customs procedures, expedite the establishment of "single windows" in border ports, and extend the practice of juxtaposed border control according to which travelers are able to go through both exit and entry procedures in the same checkpoint. Openness must respect sovereignty and territorial integrity, accommodate each country's comfort level, and refrain from imposing one's views on others or interfering in the internal affairs of other countries. Openness should follow an incremental approach, addressing more straight-forward issues before tackling more difficult ones, launching pilot projects to bring about greater progress across the board, and achieving success by accumulating small gains step by step. In this way, we can expect the Asian economy to move steadily forward on the path to greater openness, and the Asian countries to strengthen their strategic mutual trust during the process.

– We need to help the peoples of Asia to realize their dreams of happiness. Each new transport route carries on it people's dream of happiness. In stepping up connectivity in Asia, we will open more windows for more people to observe the world, pursue their dreams, and broaden their path from poverty to prosperity. In considering and planning connectivity projects, we should always put people first, heed the views of the grassroots, ensure a higher income for them, and earnestly address such practical problems as providing electricity, drinking water, medical care, schooling, employment and access to the internet. At the same time, we must protect the environment and ecosystem, so that countries can be both prosperous and beautiful.

We need to draw our peoples closer to one another for exchanges of ideas and inter-cultural dialogue, so that they will meet and learn about each other, trust and respect each other, create a harmonious and peaceful life for their common enjoyment, and jointly pursue an Asian dream of peace, prosperity and progress.

– We need to create a platform of cooperation that is

Asian in nature. Much pioneering and fundamental work on Asian connectivity has been done by international and regional organizations, and important results have been achieved. We deeply cherish and appreciate these efforts. I hope that the various mechanisms in existence will join the Asian countries to form synergy through effective coordination on the base of reality in Asia. As circumstances change, we also need to be ready to create new institutions and mechanisms.

Last month in Beijing, more than 20 Asian countries signed the inter-governmental MOU on the establishment of the Asian Infrastructure Investment Bank (AIIB). This is a major breakthrough in Asian financial cooperation. As a useful supplement to the World Bank, the Asian Development Bank, and other financial institutions, the AIIB will play a significant role in building connectivity in Asia.

Dear colleagues,

Friends,

Last fall I made a proposal on behalf of the Chinese government to build the Silk Road Economic Belt and the 21st Century Maritime Silk Road (the Belt and Road Initiative). The international community, and leaders present here in particular, have responded to the initiative positively. The initiative and the connectivity endeavor are compatible and mutually reinforcing. If the Belt and Road are likened to the two wings of a soaring Asia, then connectivity represents its arteries and veins. With the implementation of the initiative now entering a stage of pragmatic cooperation, I wish to propose the following:

First, we should focus on Asian countries and realize connectivity in Asia first. The Belt and Road both trace their origins to Asia. They will find support in Asia and bring benefit to Asia. It is natural that we focus our attention on connectivity between Asian countries and strive to expand our common interests. The Belt and Road Initiative represents a joint undertaking by China and its Asian neighbors. China gives top priority to neighboring countries in its foreign policy and pursues amity, sincerity, mutual benefit and inclusiveness in building relations with them. China is ready to provide more public goods to its Asian neighbors through connectivity, and welcomes them to board China's train of development.

Second, we should develop a basic framework of Asian connectivity by leveraging economic corridors. Now, China has made a basic master plan for the Belt and Road Initiative. It includes the land and maritime economic corridors, which are still under development, on the basis of full consultation among all parties. The proposed framework should accommodate the needs of all relevant countries and cover both land and sea-related projects. The framework, once developed, will be both extensive and inclusive, and it will have far-reaching impacts. China is ready to engage in further consultation with the countries involved with a view to improving the blueprint and laying a more solid foundation for our cooperation.

Third, we should gather an early harvest in Asian connectivity by making breakthroughs in transport infrastructure. The Silk Road project begins with roads. With roads in place, people and goods can flow. China attaches great importance to the railway and highway projects linking China to Pakistan, Bangladesh, Myanmar, Laos, Cambodia, Mongolia, Tajikistan and other neighboring countries. These projects will be given priority in the planning and implementation of the Belt and Road Initiative. The more and the sooner people benefit from the initiative, the greater appeal and vigor the initiative will have.

Fourth, we should break through bottlenecks in Asian connectivity by building a financing platform. Most Asian countries are developing countries facing a shortage of funds for development. What is important is to use what is available effectively and spend the increment wisely, so that precious financial resources will be channeled to the most worthy projects. Here, I would like to announce that China has decided to commit US$40 billion to the establishment of a Silk Road Fund. This new fund is designed to provide investment and financing support to countries along the Belt and Road for connectivity projects such as infrastructure, resources development, and industrial and financial cooperation. The Silk Road Fund is an open fund which allows establishment of sub-funds by the region, sector or project. Investors from both within and outside of Asia are welcome to participate in the Fund.

Fifth, we should strengthen the social foundation for Asian connectivity by promoting people-to-people exchanges. China welcomes dialogue between civilizations and faiths, encourages exchanges between cultures and peoples among all countries, stands in favor of joint applications for World Cultural Heritage status by all countries along the Belt and Road, and wishes to see closer cooperation between local governments of provinces and cities in Asian countries. Asia boasts a wealth of resources in the field of tourism. As our citizens travel abroad in increasing numbers, we should incorporate the Silk Road into our tourism strategies and combine our cooperation in tourism with our efforts for better connectivity. Connectivity requires great numbers of professionals. In the coming five years, China will provide neighboring countries with training opportunities for 20,000 connectivity professionals in support of their efforts to cultivate their own experts. China is also ready to send more students and scholars to neighboring countries for studies and academic exchanges.

Dear colleagues,

Friends,

A Chinese proverb says that people who cherish the same ideals follow the same path. Let us aspire towards the highest and the best, while keeping our feet firmly planted on the ground. Let us create a deeper partnership in connectivity. Let us upgrade Asia's regional cooperation and work together to build a community of common development and shared future.

Thank you!

Shape the Future
Through Asia-Pacific Partnership*

November 11, 2014

Dear colleagues,

I am very glad to meet you at Yanqi Lake in Beijing. Let me first extend a warm welcome to all of you.

Every year, flocks of swan geese fly here and stay on the lake in spring and autumn, hence Yanqi Lake, which means the lake of swan geese. We 21 member economies of APEC are just like 21 swan geese. Two lines from an ancient Chinese poem read: "The wind breaks waves into thousands of flowers on the river; flocks of swans fly across the blue sky with their wings spread." We are meeting here at Yanqi Lake to enhance cooperation and to shape a new vision for the development of the Asia-Pacific region.

This year marks the 25th anniversary of APEC. The past 25 years of APEC's growth have witnessed developing prosperity in the Asia-Pacific region. APEC has been witness to the region's historic achievements, which, in turn, have given APEC a new mission.

---

* Opening speech at the 22nd APEC Economic Leaders' Meeting in Beijing.

The world economic recovery still faces many unpredictable and uncertain factors. The Asia-Pacific region has entered a new stage of development, facing both opportunities and challenges. How to tackle the risk of fragmentation in regional economic cooperation? How to create new growth momentum in the post-financial crisis period? How to remove the financing bottlenecks hindering connectivity? These are issues we need to consider and actively address.

In the face of new conditions, we need to intensify regional economic integration and foster an open environment that is conducive to long-term development. APEC should play a leading and coordinating role in breaking through various shackles, and unleash a new round of greater openness, exchange and integration at a higher level, in broader areas and at a deeper level. We need to open the closed doors within the Asia-Pacific region and open our region fully to the rest of the world. While continuing to advance the Bogor Goals, we should vigorously promote the Free Trade Area of the Asia-Pacific (FTAAP) by identifying targets and laying out directions and road maps. This will help to realize the early completion of a highly open integration arrangement that spans across the two sides of the Pacific Ocean.

In the face of new conditions, we need to vigorously promote reform and innovation, create new growth areas and driving forces, and ensure strong and sustainable growth. Where does growth momentum come from in the post-financial crisis period? Undoubtedly, it can only come from reform, innovation and readjustment. We need to be innovative in our approach to development, pursue development through innovation and reform, and generate internal growth momentum through structural adjustment rather than driving it in the traditional manner by relying on factors of production and export. We need to change the model of market regulation, allowing the market to play a decisive role in resource allocation and improving the role of government. We need to advance scientific and technological innovation to revolutionize energy use and consumption, and make the Asia-Pacific region a global leader in new technology. This year, we have promoted cooperation in internet economy, the blue economy, and urbanization, and discussed ways of hurdling the middle-income trap, and we have made a good start in addressing all these major and urgent issues in the global economy.

In the face of new conditions, we need to accelerate our efforts to upgrade infrastructure and build comprehensive connectivity. Connectivity is about connecting physical structures. Our cooperation should extend to wherever roads, railways, air routes and the internet take us. Connectivity is about connecting rules and regulations. When coordination and cooperation are enhanced and regulatory obstacles are reduced, logistics will become smoother and exchanges more convenient. Connectivity is also about connecting the hearts of people. With enhanced mutual understanding, we can achieve better communication and be more successful in our endeavors. In short, to achieve comprehensive connectivity in the Asia-Pacific, we should bring together all member economies on both sides of the Pacific by connecting physical structures, rules and regulations, and the hearts of people. We should eliminate obstacles in accessing affordable financing, strengthen public-private partnerships, and achieve interconnected development.

Dear colleagues,

We are all APEC members. It meets the common interests of us all to foster an open economy in the Asia-Pacific featuring innovative development, interconnected growth, and converging interests. To achieve this goal, all the economies in the region need to work together to build an Asia-Pacific partnership of mutual trust, inclusiveness, cooperation, and win-win progress, and this will inject new energy into the economic development of both the Asia-Pacific and the wider world.

First, we should join together in charting the course for future development of the Asia-Pacific – it is vital to the interests of every APEC member. Having reached consensus on launching the process of the FTAAP, promoting connectivity, and pursuing innovative growth, we should now translate that consensus into action. We should draw up the development blueprint for the next 5, 10 or even 25 years and implement it step by step.

Second, we should meet global challenges as one. In the post-financial crisis period, we need to focus on the core task of sustaining growth and enhance macro policy coordination. We should also effectively address global issues such as epidemics, food security, and energy security. We should know each other better through sharing of information, share best practices through exchange of experience, facilitate collective actions through consultation and coordination, and boost regional cooperation through mutual assistance.

Third, we should work together to build cooperation platforms. Partnership means pitching in together on common goals and major initiatives. We should build APEC into an institutional platform for promoting integration, a policy platform based on experience sharing, an open platform against trade protectionism, a development platform to intensify economic and technical cooperation, and a communication platform for boosting connectivity. A stronger and more dynamic APEC is possible only with support from all its members.

I wish to announce here that China will donate US$10 million to support APEC in building its institution and capability, and in conducting practical cooperation in various fields.

Fourth, we should all pursue interconnected development. Partnership also means win-win cooperation and mutual learning. Some developing economies in the Asia-Pacific are now facing difficulties. If they cannot achieve individual development, wider development of the whole Asia-Pacific will not be sustainable. We need to increase financial and technical support to developing members, give full rein to the diversity among the Asia-Pacific economies, draw on each other's strengths, better leverage the amplifying effects of interconnected actions, and achieve common development.

Over the next three years, the Chinese government will provide 1,500 training opportunities to APEC developing members in support of capacity-building projects in trade, investment and other fields.

Dear colleagues,

Under the theme of "Shape the Future Through Asia-Pacific Partnership", we will discuss three important topics — advancing regional economic integration, promoting innovative development, economic reform and growth, and strengthening comprehensive development in infrastructure and connectivity. I am confident that our meeting today will inject new vitality into the long-term development of the Asia-Pacific region.

A single flower does not herald spring; a lone swan goose cannot make a flock. Let us take Yanqi Lake as the new starting point, and lead the swan geese of the global economy to soar higher in the vast blue sky.

Thank you!

Implement the Free Trade Zone Strategy[*]

December 5, 2014

Standing at a new starting point in history, to achieve the Two Centenary Goals and the Chinese Dream of national rejuvenation, we must adapt ourselves to the new trends of economic globalization, correctly evaluate the changing international situation, thoroughly understand the new demands in domestic reform and development, take more effective action to drive opening up to a higher level, and quicken the pace of implementing the free trade zone (FTZ) strategy and building an open economic system. We must take more initiative to further promote opening up to the outside world in a bid to boost economic development and win the international competition.

Accelerating the implementation of the FTZ strategy is an important element of a new round of opening up. The 17th CPC National Congress in 2007 listed the development of FTZs as a national strategy; the 18th CPC National Congress in 2012 required quickening the pace of implementing the FTZ strategy. The Third Plenary Session of the 18th

* Main points of the speech at the 19th group study session of the Political Bureau of the 18th CPC Central Committee.

CPC Central Committee in 2013 required that we accelerate the implementation of the FTZ strategy with neighboring countries as the basis, and create a global, high-standard FTZ network. The purpose of this group study session of the Political Bureau is to analyze the domestic and international situations we are facing and discuss how to speed up the implementation of the FTZ strategy.

We should correctly understand all new trends in economic globalization and the new demands of opening up at home. Expanding and advancing opening up, and promoting reform and development through opening up, is a powerful instrument through which China can achieve continuing progress. Opening up brings progress, while isolation leads to backwardness. International development and China's development both prove this to be true. Since the 18th CPC National Congress, we have taken the opportunity to speed up building an open economic system, and now a higher-level pattern of opening up is taking shape.

A multilateral trading regime and regional trade arrangements are the two drivers for economic globalization. Now the global trade system is undergoing the largest round of reconstruction since the 1994 Uruguay Round negotiations. China is an active participant in and firm supporter of economic globalization, and also a major contributor and beneficiary. As China's economic development has entered a new normal, in order to address the difficulties and challenges in social and economic development, we should open wider to the outside world. As a Chinese saying goes, "Opportunities are rare and hard to grasp, and easy to lose." We must size up the situation if we are to seize the critical opportunities offered by economic globalization.

Accelerating the implementation of the FTZ strategy is an objective requirement for adapting to the new trends of economic globalization. It is the option we must choose if we are to achieve deeper reform and build an open economic system, and it is an important measure in addressing foreign relations and implementing foreign strategies. We should therefore move forward at a quicker pace, and allow the FTZs to facilitate trade investments, so as to expand international markets for Chinese enterprises, and inject new energy into and open new space for China's economic development.

They provide an important platform for China to participate in the formulation of international trade rules, and to acquire the institutional power for global economic governance. Therefore, we should not be a bystander or follower, but a participant and leader. We should enhance our international competitiveness by developing FTZs, giving China a greater voice and injecting more Chinese elements in the formulation of international rules, so as to protect and expand the interests of China's development.

Accelerating the implementation of the FTZ strategy is a complicated project. We should enhance top-level design and overall planning, planning for each individual step and the overall situation, build a global FTZ network with neighboring countries as the basis and radiating out through the Belt and Road, and negotiate with the countries and regions involved in the Belt and Road Initiative on establishing FTZs, thereby ensuring closer cooperation, more effective communication, and a closer union of interests between China and the countries and regions involved in the Belt and Road Initiative. We should increase the number and improve the quality of FTZs, try out bold initiatives and keep pace with the times, open the service industry wider to the outside world, and quicken negotiations in new fields. We should stay true to our principles, improve risk evaluation and guard against risks, promote pilot projects to confirm their worth, establish an integrative system to improve supervision, and build a safety network. We should continue to improve our own capability and do our own jobs well, accelerate market-oriented reforms, build a law-based business environment, quicken the pace of economic restructuring, promote industrial upgrading, encourage enterprises to expand business and become stronger, and improve our international competitiveness and the ability to withstand risks.

We should establish fair, inclusive, and transparent market rules, and improve the international competitiveness of our service industry. We should integrate the strategies of "bringing in" and "going global", improve our foreign investment system and policies, tap the foreign investment potential of Chinese enterprises, and be courageous in and adept at allocating resources and expanding markets in a global context. We should accelerate the transition from a large to a major trading power, consolidate our traditional strengths in foreign trade, foster new competitive edges, expand the development space of foreign trade, and increase imports. We should build a strategic mentality and a global vision, and review the development of China and the world from the height of integrating the overall situations at home and abroad, pushing forward opening up.

China Welcomes All Countries Along the Routes and in Asia to Develop the Belt and Road*

March 28, 2015

We have only one planet, and countries share one world. To do well, Asia and the world cannot do without each other. Facing the fast-changing international and regional landscapes, we must see the whole picture, follow the trends of our times, and jointly build a regional order that is more favorable to Asia and the world. Through efforts towards a community of shared future for Asia, we should promote a global community of shared future. I wish to take this opportunity to share with you my thoughts on this vision.

– To build a community of shared future, we need to make sure that all countries respect one another and treat each other as equals. Countries may differ in size, strength, or level of development, but they are all equal members of the international community with an equal right to participate in regional and international affairs. On matters that

---

* Part of the keynote speech, titled "Towards a Community of Common Destiny and a New Future for Asia", at the Boao Forum for Asia Annual Conference 2015.

involve us all, we should discuss and look for a solution together. Being a major country means shouldering greater responsibilities for regional and world peace and development, as opposed to seeking greater monopoly over regional and world affairs.

To respect one another and treat each other as equals, countries must first and foremost respect other countries' social systems and development paths of their own choice, respect each other's core interests and major concerns, and have objective and rational perception of other countries' growing strength and policies. Efforts should be made to seek common ground while setting aside differences, and better still to increase common interests and dissolve differences. Our hard-won peace and stability in Asia and the region's sound momentum for development should be upheld by all. All of us must oppose interference in other countries' internal affairs and reject attempts to destabilize the region out of selfish motives.

– To build a community of shared future, we need to seek mutually beneficial cooperation and common development. Our friends in Southeast Asia say that the lotus flowers grow taller as the water rises. Our friends in Africa say that if you want to go fast, walk alone; and if you want to go far, walk together. Our friends in Europe say that a single tree cannot block the chilly wind. And Chinese people say that when big rivers have water, the small ones are filled; and when small rivers have water, the big ones are filled. All these sayings speak to one same truth, that is, only through mutually beneficial cooperation can we make significant and sustainable achievements that are beneficial to all. The old mindset of zero-sum game should give way to a new approach of win-win and all-win cooperation. The interests of others must be accommodated while pursuing one's own interests, and common development must be promoted while seeking one's own development. The vision of mutually beneficial cooperation not only applies to the field of economics, but also to politics, security, culture and many others. It applies not only to countries within the region, but also to countries from outside the region. We should enhance coordination of macro-economic policies to prevent negative spillover effects that may arise from policy changes in individual economies. We should actively promote reform of global economic governance, uphold an open world economy, and jointly respond to risks and challenges in the world economy.

China and ASEAN countries will join hands in building an even closer China-ASEAN community of shared future. The building of an East Asia economic community for ASEAN, China, Japan and ROK will be completed in 2020. We should actively build a free trade cooperation network in Asia and strive to conclude negotiations on an upgraded China-ASEAN FTA and on Regional Comprehensive Economic Partnership (RCEP) in 2015. In advancing economic integration in Asia, we need to remain committed to open regionalism and press forward with transregional cooperation, including APEC, in a coordinated manner.

We will promote a system of regional financial cooperation, explore a platform for exchanges and cooperation among Asian financial institutions, and advance complementary and coordinated development between the Asian Infrastructure Investment Bank (AIIB) and other multilateral financial institutions such as the Asian Development Bank and the World Bank. We will strengthen practical cooperation in currency stability, investment and financing, and credit rating, make progress in building institutions for the Chiang Mai Initiative Multilateralization, and build a regional financial security network. We will work towards an energy cooperation mechanism in Asia to ensure energy security.

China proposes that plans be formulated regarding connectivity in East Asia and Asia at large to advance full integration in infrastructure, policies and institutions, and personnel flow. We should increase maritime connectivity, establish a maritime cooperation mechanism in Asia, and step up cooperation in the marine economy, environmental protection, disaster management, and fisheries. In this way we can turn the seas of Asia into seas of peace, friendship and cooperation for Asian countries.

– To build a community of shared future, we need to pursue common, comprehensive, cooperative and sustainable security. In today's world, security means much more than it did before, and its implications go well beyond a single region or time frame. All sorts of factors could have a bearing on a country's security. As people of all countries share a common destiny and become increasingly interdependent, no country can have its own security guaranteed without the security of other countries or of the wider world. The Cold War mentality should truly be discarded and new security concepts be nurtured as we explore a path for Asia that ensures security of all, by all and for all.

We believe that all countries are entitled to take an equal part in regional security affairs, and all are obliged to work to ensure security for the region. The legitimate security concerns of each country need to be respected and guaranteed. At the same time, in handling security issues in Asia, it is important to bear in mind both the history and reality of Asia, take a multi-pronged and holistic approach, improve coordinated regional security governance, and safeguard security in both the traditional and non-traditional realms. It is important to conduct dialogue and cooperation to enhance security at national and regional levels, and to increase cooperation as the way to safeguard peace and security. It is important to resolve disputes through peaceful means, and oppose the willful threat or use of force. Security should be given the same emphasis as development, and sustainable development surely provides a way to sustainable security. Countries in Asia need to step up cooperation with countries and organizations outside the region, and all parties are welcome to play a positive and constructive role in upholding development and security in Asia.

– To build a community of shared future, we need to ensure inclusiveness and mutual learning among civilizations. Over the past millennia, history has witnessed ancient civilizations appear and thrive along the Yellow and Yangtze rivers, the Indus, the Ganges, the Euphrates, and the Tigris River, as well as in Southeast Asia, each adding its own splendor to the progress of human civilization. Today, Asia proudly maintains its distinct diversity and still nurtures all those civilizations, ethnic groups and religions in this grand Asian family.

Mencius, a great philosopher of ancient China, said: "Things are born to be different." Civilizations are unique, and no one is superior to the others. There needs to be more exchange and dialogue among civilizations and development models, so that each can draw on the strength of the other and all can thrive and prosper by way of mutual learning and common development. Let us promote inter-civilization exchanges to build bridges of friendship for our people, drive human development and safeguard world peace.

China proposes that a conference of dialogue among Asian civilizations be held to provide a platform for enhancing interactions among youth, NGOs, local communities, and the media, and for forming a network of think-tank cooperation, so as to add to Asian people's rich cultural life and contribute to more vibrant regional cooperation and development.

Right now, the Chinese people are working in unison to establish a moderately prosperous society in all respects, further reform, advance the rule of law, and strengthen Party discipline. Our objective is to realize the Two Centenary

Goals for China's development and to realize the Chinese Dream of national rejuvenation. I wish to use this opportunity to reaffirm China's commitment to the path of peaceful development, and to cooperation and common development in the Asia-Pacific. China will be firm in its resolve and all its policies will be designed to achieve such a purpose.

Now, the Chinese economy has entered a phase of new normal. It is shifting gear from high speed to medium-to-high speed growth, from an extensive model that emphasized scale and speed to a more intensive one emphasizing quality and efficiency, and from being driven by investment in production factors to being driven by innovation. China's economy grew by 7.4 percent in 2014, with a 7 percent increase in labor productivity and a 4.8 percent fall in energy intensity. The share of domestic consumption in GDP rose, the services sector expanded at a faster pace, and efficiency and quality continued to improve. When looking at China's economy, one should not focus on growth rate only. As the economy continues to grow in size, around 7 percent growth would be quite impressive, and the momentum it generates would be larger than growth at double digits in previous years. It is fair to say that the Chinese economy is highly resilient and has much potential, which gives us sufficient room to leverage a host of policy tools. Having said that, China will continue to be responsive to new trends, and to take the initiative to shape the new normal in our favor. We will focus on improving quality and efficiency, and give even greater priority to shifting the growth model and adjusting the economic structure. We will make further solid efforts to boost economic development and drive deeper reform and opening up. We will take further steps to unleash the creativity and ingenuity of the people, to be more effective in safeguarding social fairness and justice, to raise people's living standards, and to make sure that China's economic and social development are both sound and steady.

This new normal of the Chinese economy will continue to present more opportunities in trade, growth, investment, and cooperation for other countries in Asia and beyond. In the coming five years, China will import more than US$10 trillion of goods, Chinese investment abroad will exceed US$500 billion, and more than 500 million outbound visits will be made by Chinese tourists. China will stick to its basic state policy of opening up, improve its investment climate, and protect the lawful rights and interests of investors. I believe that together, the people of Asian countries can drive the train of Asia's development to an even brighter future.

What China needs most is a harmonious and stable domestic environment and a peaceful international environment. Turbulence and war run against the fundamental interests of the Chinese people. The Chinese nation loves peace and has, since ancient times, held in high esteem such philosophies as "harmony is the most valuable", "peace and harmony should prevail" and "all men under heaven are brothers". In the recent past China itself suffered from turbulence and war for more than a century, and the Chinese people would never want to inflict the same tragedy on other countries or peoples. History teaches us that no country that tries to achieve its goals with force has ever succeeded. China will be steadfast in pursuing an independent foreign policy of peace, the path of peaceful development, the mutually beneficial strategy of opening up, and the approach of upholding the greater good and pursuing shared interests. China will work to promote a new model of international relations based on win-win cooperation, and will always remain a staunch force for world peace and common development.

Close neighbors are better than distant relatives. This is a simple truth that the Chinese people got to know in ancient times. That explains China's firm commitment to building friendship and partnership with its neighbors to foster an amicable, secure and prosperous neighborhood. Under the principles of amity, sincerity, mutual benefit and inclusiveness, China is working actively to strengthen win-win cooperation and connectivity with its neighbors and bring them even more benefit through its own development. China has signed treaties of good-neighborliness, friendship and cooperation with eight of its neighbors and is holding discussions to sign a similar treaty with ASEAN. China stands ready to sign such treaties with all its neighbors to provide strong support for the development of bilateral relations as well as prosperity and stability in the region.

In 2013, during my visits to Kazakhstan and Indonesia,

I proposed building a Silk Road Economic Belt and a 21st Century Maritime Silk Road. The Belt and Road Initiative, meeting the development needs of China, countries along the routes and the region at large, will serve the common interests of relevant parties and answer the call of our time for regional and global cooperation.

In promoting this initiative, China will follow the principles of extensive consultation, joint contribution, and shared benefits. Development projects will be open and inclusive, not exclusive. There will be a genuine "chorus" comprising all countries along the routes, not a "solo" performance on the part of China. To develop the Belt and Road is not to replace existing mechanisms or initiatives for regional cooperation. Quite the contrary, we will build on the existing basis to help countries align their development strategies and form synergy. Currently, more than 60 countries along the routes and international organizations have shown interest in taking part in the development of the Belt and Road. The Belt and Road and the AIIB are both open initiatives. We welcome all countries along the routes and in Asia, as well as our friends and partners around the world, to take an active part in these endeavors.

The Belt and Road Initiative is no rhetoric. It represents real work that will be seen and felt and will bring real benefits to countries in the region. Thanks to the concerted efforts of all parties, the Vision and Actions paper of the initiative has already been developed. Substantive progress has been made in the establishment of the AIIB. The Silk Road

Fund has been launched, and a number of infrastructure connectivity projects are moving forward. These early fruits bear testimony to the broad prospects of the Belt and Road Initiative.

China's Development Provides New Cooperation Opportunities for Other Countries and Foreign Companies*

March 29, 2015

As China's economy has entered a new normal, its foreign economic cooperation is also growing, which means it is providing new cooperation opportunities for countries and other companies around the world. China is opening wider to the outside world. Our policy towards foreign investment will not change. Our protection of the legitimate rights and interests of foreign-invested enterprises will not change. And our commitment to providing better services to foreign companies in their investment and business activities in China will not change.

At present, the world economic recovery is still unstable, uncertain and unbalanced. Overall, the Asian economy has maintained rapid growth. And China's economy has entered a new normal. This is the background, and I want to hear your opinions.

---

* Main points of the remarks at a meeting with representatives of Chinese and foreign entrepreneurs attending the Boao Forum for Asia Annual Conference 2015.

China's economy is deeply integrated with the global economy and forms an important driving force of the economy of Asia and the world. The efficiency and quality of China's economy are improving; there are positive adjustments to the economic structure; and major progress is being made in deeper reform and opening up with new developments. China's economy has entered a new normal and will take on a more advanced form, with a more complicated division of labor and a more appropriate structure. This is also the starting point for us to do our economic work soundly. Under the new normal, the key to achieving new development and new breakthroughs lies in making comprehensive moves to further reform and advance the rule of law.

At present, China is having closer interaction with the world, with more opportunities shared and a stronger bond for a shared future. China is offering more opportunities in every sense.

More opportunities are being offered in the Chinese market. China will continue to experience robust growth for the foreseeable future, which will create huge domestic demand. The consumption of the Chinese people is further growing, and enterprises that provide safe and high-quality products and services have good prospects for the future.

More investment opportunities are being offered in China. Investment opportunities in infrastructure connectivity as well as in new technologies, new products, new forms of business, and new business models are constantly appearing.

Emerging industries, service industries and small and micro businesses are playing a more prominent role. The development of small-scale, intelligent, and specialized manufacturing is bringing about more opportunities.

More opportunities are being offered in spurring green growth in China. We shall continue on a path of green development, making resource-saving and environmental friendliness core to our work and daily lives. We are engaged in a revolution in energy production and consumption; we are optimizing our energy structure, implementing a policy of priority to energy conservation, and pushing forward energy conservation in key fields.

More opportunities are being offered in expanding foreign cooperation. We support the multilateral trading regime, commit ourselves to the Doha Round negotiations, advocate the Free Trade Area of the Asia-Pacific, promote negotiations on regional comprehensive economic partnership, advocate the establishment of the AIIB, boost all-round economic and financial cooperation, and work actively for economic globalization and regional integration.

Our initiative of building the Silk Road Economic Belt and the 21st Century Maritime Silk Road will encourage trade and investment between China and countries along the routes, promote connectivity and new models of industrialization in the Belt and Road countries, and support common development of all participating countries so that the people can enjoy the fruits of development.

We hope that the annual trade between China and other

Belt and Road countries will surpass US$2.5 trillion in a decade or so. We hope you, business leaders, will work closely together with Chinese enterprises, the Silk Road Fund and the soon to be established AIIB, create new cooperation models, and explore new approaches to expanding the market for mutual benefit. We hope that you will continue to direct your attention to China's economic development, seize opportunities provided by China, and advance together with us on China's new development journey.

Expand Common Interests,
Realize Common Prosperity*

April 21, 2015

The Chinese nation loves peace. Over 2,000 years ago, the Chinese already knew that a belligerent country, however powerful it may seem, will not prosper. "Do not do unto others what you do not want others to do unto you." This is a principle that we Chinese adhere to, and we do not subscribe to the belief that a country is bound to seek hegemony when it becomes powerful. Peaceful development is in China's interests, and also in the interests of Asia and the world. Nothing will shake our resolve to pursue peaceful development. China is committed to the principle of non-interference in other countries' internal affairs; it will never impose its own will on anyone; and China will never seek hegemony however strong it might become.

China will continue to pursue win-win cooperation and enhance friendship and cooperation with other countries. It will stay committed to the policy of amity, sincerity, mutual

---

* Part of the speech, titled "Building a China-Pakistan Community of Shared Future to Pursue Win-Win Cooperation", delivered at the Parliament of Pakistan.

benefit and inclusiveness. It will expand win-win cooperation with its neighbors so as to deliver more benefits to them
through its own development. China will remain a reliable
friend and sincere partner of other developing countries.
China will continue to open up for common benefit, and advance all-round opening up to build an open economy. This
will create new development opportunities and space for
both Asia and the world.

Building the Silk Road Economic Belt and the 21st
Century Maritime Silk Road is a significant initiative China
launched in order to open itself to the full in the new era.
The initiative also reflects China's commitment to sharing
development opportunities and outcomes with more countries. We will strengthen cooperation with countries along
the Belt and Road and realize the connectivity of roads,
trade, finance, policies and our peoples, so as to jointly
build an open platform for cooperation and create new
impetus to achieve sustainable development in the related
regions.

South Asia is where the Belt and Road meet. It is therefore a focal area and important cooperation partner for advancing the Belt and Road Initiative. Good progress has been
made in building the China-Pakistan Economic Corridor and
the Bangladesh-China-India-Myanmar Economic Corridor,
which are closely connected with the Belt and Road. These
two economic corridors will give a strong boost to the economic growth of the related countries and provide a strong
new force for deeper regional cooperation in South Asia.

Peace, development and cooperation are the themes of our great times. The vast and richly endowed South Asia has boundless potential for development. The hard-working and talented people of South Asia are making vigorous efforts to speed up development in the region and turn it into a new pole of growth for the world economy.

China is the biggest neighbor of South Asia. A peaceful, stable, and prosperous South Asia is beneficial to China's development. China is ready to pursue its development strategy in parallel with those of the South Asian countries to realize mutually beneficial development and common prosperity. During my visit to three South Asian countries last year, I put forward a number of initiatives to strengthen China's cooperation with the South Asian countries, which are being implemented. China respects the unique culture and historical traditions of the South Asian region. We are a sincere partner of South Asian countries. We will treat each other with respect and as equals, and accommodate each other's comfort level to ensure long-term and sound growth in our relationships.

Only through win-win cooperation can we expand common interests and realize common prosperity. South Asia occupies a priority on China's westward opening-up agenda, and we will share more development practices with the South Asian countries to complement each other's development endeavors. China is ready to do more to provide assistance and support to South Asian countries within the framework of South-South cooperation.

Both China and the South Asian countries have a long history, and we both value benevolence, friendship, inclusiveness, mutual learning, harmony and coexistence. China is ready to strengthen inter-civilization dialogue with South Asian countries, an important part of such dialogue across Asia, so as to jointly promote the wisdom of the East and Asian values.

It is thanks to openness, inclusiveness, unity and self-reliance that the Asian countries have succeeded in promoting development, prosperity and national renewal. We must continue to be guided by such visions to achieve greater development in the future. China will strengthen cooperation with the South Asian countries to jointly advance regional cooperation in South Asia and Asia as a whole. China will upgrade its cooperation with the South Asian Association for Regional Cooperation, and step up international coordination with the South Asian countries under multilateral frameworks to jointly uphold the interests of developing countries.

The Belt and Road Initiative Is
Open and Inclusive*

September 22, 2015

As far as the existing international system is concerned, China has been a participant, builder and contributor. We stand firmly behind the international order and system that is based on the purposes and principles of the UN Charter. A great number of countries, especially developing countries, want to see a more just and equitable international system, but this does not mean that they want to unravel the entire system or start all over again. Rather, what they want is to reform and improve the system to keep up with the times. This would serve the common interests of all countries and humanity as a whole.

China has benefited from the international community in its own development, and China in turn should contribute to global development. Our Belt and Road Initiative, our establishment of the Silk Road Fund and our proposal to set up the AIIB are all aimed at helping the common development of all countries rather than seeking any kind of spheres of

---

* Part of the speech at a reception held jointly by the local government and friendly groups in Seattle, Washington State, the United States.

political influence. The Belt and Road Initiative is open and inclusive. We welcome the participation of all countries, the US included, and international organizations. We have vigorously promoted economic integration in the Asia-Pacific region and worked to realize the goal of establishing the Free Trade Area of the Asia-Pacific, because we want to help to shape a free, open, convenient and dynamic space for development in the Asia-Pacific region. We call for an outlook of common, comprehensive, cooperative and sustainable security, because we want to work with other countries in the region and the rest of the international community to maintain peace and security in the Asia-Pacific region.

New Vision of the Silk Road, Actions for Common Development*

October 15, 2015

Themed on "New Vision of the Silk Road, Actions for Common Development", the conference is of practical importance as it offers an opportunity for in-depth exchanges and dialogue on pushing forward the Belt and Road Initiative. Speeding up the building of the Belt and Road will promote economic prosperity and regional cooperation among the countries along the routes, facilitate exchanges and mutual learning among different civilizations, and enhance peace and development of the world. It is a great cause that will benefit the participating countries and their peoples. I believe that this special conference will contribute to advancing the Belt and Road Initiative and boosting common development.

Over the past two years the Belt and Road Initiative has been warmly welcomed by the international community, especially by the 60-plus countries along the routes, and it is

---

* Main points of the speech when meeting with foreign representatives attending the Asian Political Parties' Special Conference on the Silk Road in Beijing.

producing early results. Upholding the principles of extensive consultation, joint contribution, and shared benefits, the initiative is open and inclusive and advocates mutual learning. It strives to achieve mutual benefit, win-win outcomes, and common development. It puts people first and works in their interests. So it will bring tangible benefits to the peoples of all the countries along the routes.

Political parties and political leaders should be visionaries who take on the responsibilities required by the times, and spearhead the joint effort in building the Belt and Road. We should aim high in our work, and be pragmatic. By aiming high we must follow the trends of the times and be good designers at the top level. By pragmatic we must propel the initiative in an orderly fashion for early results. While strengthening dialogue and communication, we should also enhance strategic connectivity. In the light of each country's progress in reform and development, we should engage in honest dialogue on the Belt and Road Initiative and come up with measures for cooperation. We should take action to make our voices heard, and pool strength from all sources. Political parties and political leaders should take the lead in guiding, coordinating and organizing political forces, think tanks, the media, industrial and businesses, and NGOs to communicate and cooperate under the BRI framework, so as to create a favorable environment in terms of politics, business, and public opinion.

Advancing the Belt and Road Initiative is an important part of China's 13th Five-year Plan (2016-2020). China will continue to be a good neighbor and partner of adjoining countries; we will continue to foster an amicable, secure and prosperous neighborhood, and pursue a foreign policy of amity, sincerity, mutual benefit, and inclusiveness towards our neighbors. All are welcome to board China's express train of development for common growth.

Belt and Road: A Wide, Open Thoroughfare for All of Us[*]

October 21, 2015

The current global economy is highly volatile. However, the more uncertain the prospects, the more we need confidence. Historical experiences and the laws of economics tell us that the global economy can never enjoy untroubled development, but growth is after all the general trend and it will not be changed by temporary rises and falls in data or by short-term market fluctuations.

The overall European economy enjoys stable prospects. We believe that Europe will achieve new development and progress through its own wisdom and efforts. Some emerging markets are seeing slower economic growth and certain countries are facing relatively greater difficulties and challenges. However, after decades of rapid development, emerging markets – with bigger economic aggregate, more tenacity, and more solid economic foundations – still enjoy sound economic fundamentals and therefore will continue to serve as a powerful propeller of global economic growth.

---

[*] Main points of the speech at the China-UK Business Summit in the City of London.

As the biggest emerging market, China has entered a new normal in economic development. Global economic development is now facing more difficulties and against such a background, China's economy grew by 6.9 percent in the first three quarters this year, continuing to play a vital role in driving global economic growth. At present, China's economy maintains an overall stable performance, with progress being made in keeping steady growth, promoting reform, adjusting the economic structure, improving people's living standards, and fending off risks. The main indicators are within a reasonable range and in line with expected targets. Economically China does face some downward pressure and certain structural problems, but it is a normal adjustment the economy has to go through when its growth reaches a certain stage and level. We will continue pushing steady growth, promoting reform, adjusting the economic structure, improving people's living standards, and fending off risks to promote sustainable and sound economic development. We will continue pursuing a mutually beneficial strategy of opening up and seek growth as a part of global prosperity and development.

The new era requires new thinking. The implementation of the Belt and Road Initiative will bring huge development opportunities for China and countries along the routes. The Belt and Road Initiative is open and serves as a "circle of friends" crossing Africa and linking the Eurasian continent, a great circle that every country with an interest can join in. The initiative is diverse and covers all cooperation fields and various cooperation approaches. It is a gigantic win-win program with the participation of all countries aimed at achieving common development and prosperity by following the principles of extensive consultation, joint contribution, and shared benefits. Indeed, the Belt and Road is not a private, exclusive road but a wide, open thoroughfare for all of us.

China and the UK enjoy high complementarity in the industrial structure, share similar vision of open markets, and have the common wish to promote free trade and expand two-way investment. Bilateral cooperation within the BRI framework enjoys promising prospects and huge potential. I have a 4-point proposal to open up a new front for bilateral cooperation.

First, boost mutual trust with earnest effort and solid measures. Bilateral cooperation is based on mutual political trust, and all cooperation will be groundless without mutual trust. During my visit, the two countries decided to establish a comprehensive strategic partnership oriented to the 21st century world, which charts the course for all-round China-UK cooperation in the coming 5-10 years and will surely bring our bilateral cooperation onto a track of fast development.

Second, seek complementarity in policy coordination. The two countries should deepen cooperation by improving complementarity in our development strategies and industrial policies. China welcomes capital, technology and talent from the UK to participate in the Belt and Road Initiative, the 13th Five-year Plan, the Internet Plus strategy and the Made in China 2025. To this end, China is willing to offer relevant policy information and a sound investment environment to UK enterprises. The UK government has also proposed the UK Industry 2050 strategy which highly accords with China's development strategy and industrial policy and therefore will generate huge opportunities for bilateral cooperation.

Third, pursue tangible results in cooperation programs. Only tangible results from bilateral cooperation can benefit the two peoples. Our two countries should earnestly advance such major projects as nuclear power, high-speed rail, and infrastructure construction, and push for an early launch of these landmark cooperation projects. We should set up a long-term mechanism to deepen subnational cooperation in economy and trade. China hopes to advance the Renminbi internationalization process in London and Europe, and will continue to support the development of an offshore Renminbi market in London and enhance cooperation with the UK in multilateral financial institutions, including the International Monetary Fund, the World Bank and the Asian Infrastructure Investment Bank. China will boost cooperation between small and medium-sized enterprises in our two countries and encourage Chinese enterprises to invest overseas; we also welcome more UK enterprises to invest and do business in China. We hope that the UK will continue to provide a sound and convenient investment environment for Chinese enterprises.

Fourth, develop new ways of cooperation. We should advance bilateral cooperation in emerging industries and carry out mutually beneficial cooperation between China's seven major strategic emerging industries and the UK's eight major technological and strategic industries. In carrying out bilateral cooperation, enterprises of both countries can also conduct third-party cooperation and jointly develop the international market. China will hold further discussions with the UK on tapping into our respective strengths to help the development of countries in Asia, Africa, Latin America and other regions based on the demand, consent and participation of third parties. Our two countries should take into consideration all factors and evaluate different investment, financing and operation models such as the Public-Private-Partnership and Build-Operate-Transfer in a proper way, so as to adopt desired operating models, complement each other's strengths, maximize the economic and social results of bilateral cooperation, and bring benefit to our two peoples.

The Belt and Road Initiative Is a Strategic Measure to Boost Opening Up and Promote Economic Diplomacy*

October 29, 2015

Open development prioritizes interactions between China and the international community. Profound changes are taking place in international economic cooperation and competition, and major adjustments are under way in the global economic governance system and rules. Global communication is becoming more profound, more extensive, and more frequent, and the pressure to cope with external economic risks and maintain national economic security is unprecedented.

Our problem now is not whether to continue opening up, but how to improve the quality of opening up and increase China's connectivity with others. We are not opening up wide enough; we lack the ability to use domestic and foreign markets and resources; we are weak in dealing with international trade friction, in exerting influence on the international economy, and in applying international trade

---

* Part of the speech at the second full assembly of the Fifth Plenary Session of the 18th CPC Central Committee.

113

rules. We need to improve in these areas. To this end, we must uphold the basic national policy of opening up, implement an opening-up strategy characterized by mutual benefit, strengthen cultural exchange, and improve the layout of opening-up regions, of foreign trade, and of investment. With such efforts we can form a new system for opening up, develop an open economy at a higher level, and drive innovation, reform and development.

The Belt and Road Initiative is a major strategic measure to boost opening up and provide a top-level design for economic diplomacy. We should identify areas where breakthroughs are most likely, promote our experience to wider areas and consolidate progress step by step to achieve final success. We should help to improve the global economic governance system, play a leading role in developing the global economic agenda, maintain a multilateral trading regime, speed up implementation of the FTZ strategy, and actively undertake our international responsibilities and obligations commensurate with our ability and status.

A New Era of China-Africa Cooperation and Common Development[*]

December 4, 2015

The world is undergoing profound changes. Economic globalization and information technology have helped greatly release social productivity. We have been presented with unprecedented opportunities for development. On the other hand, we are faced with unprecedented challenges, as hegemony, terrorism, financial turbulence and environmental crisis have become more pronounced.

In conducting China's relations with Africa, we apply the principles of sincerity, affinity, and good faith and uphold the values of the greater good and shared interests. We will work with our African friends to embrace a new era of mutually beneficial cooperation and common development. With this in mind, I propose that the new China-Africa strategic partnership be upgraded to a comprehensive strategic and cooperative partnership. To forge this partnership, we should strengthen the following five "major pillars".

---

* Part of the speech, titled "Open a New Era of China-Africa Win-Win Cooperation and Common Development", at the opening ceremony of the Johannesburg Summit of the Forum on China-Africa Cooperation.

First, we should remain committed to political equality and mutual trust. A high degree of mutual trust is the foundation of China-Africa friendship. We should respect each other's choice of development path, and neither of us should try to impose one's will on the other. On issues involving the core interests and major concerns of either side, we should jointly uphold equity and justice in the spirit of mutual understanding and mutual support. China strongly believes that Africa belongs to the African people and that African affairs should be decided by the African people.

Second, we should remain committed to mutually beneficial economic cooperation. We Chinese value friendship and justice as well as shared interests, and we place more importance on the former. Friendship and justice, which define China-Africa relations, require us to facilitate Africa's development efforts and ultimately deliver common development through mutually beneficial cooperation. We should fully leverage the strengths of mutual political trust and economic complementarity between China and Africa, and focus on cooperation in industrial capacity, networks of high-speed railway, expressway and regional civil aviation, and industrialization. This will enable China-Africa cooperation to develop in all areas and benefit both Chinese and African people.

Third, we should remain committed to mutually enriching cultural exchanges. Diversity makes the world beautiful. We are proud that both China and Africa have time-honored and splendid civilizations. We should strengthen cultural exchanges and mutual learning between China and Africa, and facilitate exchanges between young people, women, think tanks, the media, universities and other sectors of the two sides. We should promote cultural interaction, policy coordination and people-to-people exchanges to advance common progress and ensure lasting friendship between China and Africa from generation to generation.

Fourth, we should remain committed to mutual assistance in security. Poverty is the root cause of chaos while peace is the guarantor of development. Development holds the key to solving all problems. China supports African people in settling African issues themselves in the African way. We are of the view that in resolving security issues, both symptoms and root causes must be addressed in a holistic way. China stands ready to help Africa build the capacity to maintain and strengthen peace and security, and support Africa in its endeavors to speed up development, eradicate poverty, and realize durable peace.

Fifth, we should remain committed to solidarity and coordination in international affairs. China and Africa share a common position on and interests in a wide range of international issues. We should strengthen consultation and coordination, work for a fairer and more equitable global governance system, and safeguard our common interests. China will continue to stand up and speak for Africa at the United Nations and other forums, and support Africa in playing a greater role on the world stage.

To build a China-Africa comprehensive strategic and cooperative partnership, China will implement 10 cooperation programs with Africa in the next three years. Guided by the principles of government leadership, enterprise as the major actor, market operation, and mutually beneficial cooperation, China will introduce these programs to address three bottleneck issues holding back Africa's development, namely, inadequate infrastructure, lack of professional and skilled personnel, and shortage of capital. These programs will help accelerate Africa's industrialization and agricultural modernization, and thereby help Africa to achieve sustainable development on its own.

– The China-Africa industrialization program. China will actively promote partnering in the fields of industrial complementarity and industrial capacity between China and Africa, and encourage more Chinese enterprises to make investment in Africa. China will build or upgrade a number of industrial parks in cooperation with Africa, send senior experts and advisers to Africa, and set up regional vocational education centers and schools with a view to enhancing Africa's industrial capacity. In this context, China will also train 200,000 technical personnel and provide 40,000 training opportunities for African personnel in China.

– The China-Africa agricultural modernization program. China will share its experience in agricultural development with Africa and transfer readily applicable farming technologies. We will encourage Chinese enterprises to engage in large-scale farming, animal husbandry, and grain storage and processing in Africa to create more local jobs and increase rural incomes. China will carry out agricultural development projects in 100 African villages to raise rural living standards, send 30 teams of agricultural experts to Africa, and establish a "10+10" cooperation mechanism between Chinese and African agricultural research institutes. China is gravely concerned about the poor harvests caused by El Nino in many African countries and will provide RMB1 billion of emergency food aid to the affected countries.

– The China-Africa infrastructure program. China will step up mutually beneficial cooperation with Africa in infrastructure planning, design, construction, operation, and maintenance. We support Chinese enterprises in their active participation in Africa's infrastructural development, particularly in sectors such as railways, roads, regional aviation, ports, electricity, and telecommunications, which will help enhance Africa's capacity for sustainable development. We will help African countries in establishing five transport universities.

– The China-Africa financial program. China will expand its Renminbi settlement and currency swap operations with African countries. It will encourage Chinese financial institutions to set up more branches in Africa, and increase its investment and financing cooperation with Africa in multiple ways so as to provide financial support and services for Africa's industrialization and modernization.

– The China-Africa green development program. China will support Africa in bolstering its capacity for green, low-carbon and sustainable development and help Africa in launching 100 projects to develop clean energy, protect wildlife, promote environment-friendly agricultural projects, and build smart cities. China-Africa cooperation will never be pursued at the expense of Africa's eco-system and long-term interests.

– The China-Africa trade and investment facilitation program. China will carry out 50 aid-for-trade projects to improve Africa's "software" and "hardware" capacity for its internal and external trade and investment. China is ready to negotiate comprehensive free trade agreements with countries and regional organizations in Africa covering trade in goods and services and investment cooperation. These agreements, once concluded, will boost China's import of African products. China will support African countries in enhancing law enforcement capacity in areas such as customs, quality inspection and taxation. We will also engage in cooperation with Africa in standardization, certification and accreditation, and e-commerce.

– The China-Africa poverty reduction program. While intensifying its own poverty reduction efforts, China will increase its aid to Africa. We will carry out 200 "Happy Life" projects and poverty reduction programs focusing on women and children. We will cancel outstanding debts in the form of interest-free government loans borrowed by the least-developed African countries that would mature by the end of 2015.

– The China-Africa public health program. China will help Africa strengthen its public health prevention and control system and build up its capacity in public health, including the building of the African Center for Disease Control.

We will support pacesetting cooperation between 20 Chinese hospitals and 20 African hospitals, and upgrade hospital departments. We will continue to send medical teams to Africa and provide medical assistance, such as the "Brightness Action" program for cataract patients, and maternal and child care. We will provide more of the anti-malaria compound artemisinin to Africa, and encourage and support local drug production by Chinese enterprises in Africa to increase Africans' access to medicines.

– The China-Africa cultural and people-to-people program. China will build five cultural centers in Africa and provide satellite TV reception to 10,000 African villages. We will provide Africa with 2,000 educational opportunities with diplomas or degrees and 30,000 government scholarships. Every year, we will sponsor visits by 200 African scholars and study trips by 500 young Africans to China, and train 1,000 media professionals from Africa. We will support the opening of more direct flights between China and Africa to boost our tourism cooperation.

– The China-Africa peace and security program. China will provide a grant of US$60 million to African Union to support the building and operation of the African Standby Force and the African Capacity for the Immediate Response to Crisis. China will continue to participate in UN peace-keeping missions in Africa and support African countries in their capacity building in areas such as national defense, counter-terrorism, riot prevention, customs and immigration control.

To ensure successful implementation of these 10 co-operation programs, China has decided to provide financial support totaling US$60 billion. This includes US$5 billion of grants and interest-free loans; US$35 billion of concessional loans on more favorable terms and export credit lines; an increase of US$5 billion to the China-Africa Development Fund and the Special Loan for the Development of African SMEs respectively; and the China-Africa Fund for Industrial Cooperation with an initial contribution of US$10 billion.

This year marks the 15th anniversary of the Forum on China-Africa Cooperation (FOCAC). The past 15 years have seen fruitful progress across the board in China-Africa practical cooperation. In 2014, two-way trade and China's total non-financial investment in Africa had grown by multiples of 22 and 60 compared with the year 2000, which shows that China's contribution to Africa's economic development has risen significantly. FOCAC has become a pacesetter in China-Africa cooperation, a model of South-South cooperation, and a champion for greater international attention to and input in Africa.

China-Africa relations have today reached a stage of growth unmatched in history. We should take bold steps, scale the heights, and look afar. Let us join hands, pool the wisdom and strength of the 2.4 billion Chinese and Africans, and open a new era of China-Africa mutually beneficial co-operation and common development.

Jointly Build a Community of Shared Future in Cyberspace[*]

December 16, 2015

Cyberspace is a common space for human activities. The future of cyberspace should be in the hands of all countries. Countries should step up communication, broaden consensus, and extend cooperation to jointly build a community of shared future in cyberspace. To this end, I wish to propose five points.

First, speed up the building of global internet infrastructure and promote inter-connectivity. The essence of the internet is connectivity, and herein lies the value of information. Only when the IT infrastructure is well developed can information flow smoothly, can the digital divide between different countries, regions, and communities be narrowed, and the full flow of information resources ensured. China is now implementing the Broadband China strategy. It is estimated that by 2020, the broadband network in China will, by and large, cover every village. The "last kilometer" of internet infrastructure will be linked up thanks to this strategy,

---

* Part of the speech at the opening ceremony of the Second World Internet Conference in Wuzhen, Zhejiang Province.

and more people will have access to the internet. China stands ready to work with all parties concerned, increase investment and technical support to accelerate the building of global internet infrastructure, and enable more developing countries and their peoples to take advantage of the development opportunities brought by the internet.

Second, build an online platform for cultural exchange and mutual learning. Culture and civilization are enriched through exchange and mutual learning. The internet is an important carrier to spread the best of humanity's cultures and promote positive energy. China is ready to build, through the internet, a bridge of international cultural interaction and mutual learning for people of all countries to share the cultures of the world and their thoughts and feelings, and enhance mutual understanding. We will work with other countries to leverage the strength of the internet as a communication platform, so that people in other countries may come to know more about Chinese culture and the Chinese people can learn more of theirs. Together, we will promote the prosperity and development of cyber culture, which in turn will enrich people's minds and thoughts, and advance human civilization and progress.

Third, promote innovative development of the cyber economy for common prosperity. The world economy is on a difficult and tortuous path to recovery. The Chinese economy is also under some downward pressure. Solutions lie in innovation-driven development, which will open new horizons. China is now implementing the Internet Plus action plan, advancing the building of Digital China, developing the sharing economy, and supporting internet-based innovation in all forms, with a view to improving the quality and efficiency of development. The robust growth of the internet in China has provided a sizable market for enterprises and business starters of all countries. China's door of opening up will never close. Our policy towards foreign investment will not change. Our protection of the legitimate rights and interests of foreign-invested enterprises will not change. And our commitment to providing better services to foreign companies in their investment and business activities in China will not change. As long as they abide by China's laws, enterprises and business starters from all countries are warmly welcome to invest and do business in China. We are ready to step up cooperation with all countries. Through the development of cross-border e-commerce and the building of information economy demonstration zones, we will be able to spur the growth of worldwide investment and trade, and promote global development of the digital economy.

Fourth, maintain cyber security and promote orderly development. Security and development are like the two wings of a bird or the two wheels of a cart. Security ensures development, and development is the goal of security. Cyber security poses a global challenge. No country can distance itself or remain immune from such challenge. Maintaining cyber security is the shared responsibility of the international community. All countries should work together to contain the abuse of information technology, oppose cyber surveillance and cyber attacks, and reject an arms race in cyberspace. China will work with all other countries to step up dialogue and exchanges, and effectively manage differences. We will work with all parties for the formulation of international cyberspace rules acceptable to all parties and an international convention against terrorism in cyberspace, improve the legal support mechanism to fight cybercrime, and jointly uphold peace and security in cyberspace.

Fifth, build an internet governance system to promote fairness and justice. International cyberspace governance should feature a multilateral approach with multiparty participation. It should be based on consultation between all parties, leveraging the role of various players, including governments, international organizations, internet companies, technology communities, non-governmental institutions, and individual citizens. There can be no room for unilateralism. Decisions should not be made with one party calling the shots or only a few parties discussing among themselves. All countries should step up communication and exchange, improve dialogue and consultation mechanisms on cyberspace, and study and formulate global internet governance rules, so that the global internet governance system becomes fairer and more reasonable and reflects in a more balanced way the aspiration and interests of the majority of countries. This World Internet Conference is being held precisely for the purpose of building a platform for all to govern and benefit from the global internet, and to work together for the healthy development of the internet.

"All good principles should adapt to changing times to remain relevant." While the internet is invisible, internet users are visible. The internet is the common home of humanity. Making it better, cleaner and safer is the common responsibility of the international community. Let us work hand in hand to promote an interconnected cyberspace shared and governed by all, and contribute to a better future for the progress of all mankind.

Address at the Inauguration Ceremony of the Asian Infrastructure Investment Bank

January 16, 2016

Honorable heads of delegations,

Honorable ministers,

Distinguished guests,

Ladies and gentlemen,

Dear friends,

Now is a moment that will be recorded in history. Today, representatives from 57 countries are gathered in Beijing for the opening of the Asian Infrastructure Investment Bank (AIIB), and the inaugural ceremony of the AIIB Board of Governors and Board of Directors. On behalf of the Chinese government and people and also in my own name, let me extend a warm welcome to all guests present. I want to congratulate the AIIB on its inauguration and give my heartfelt thanks to all parties for their support and dedication to the founding of the AIIB.

The initiative to set up the AIIB was put forward by China in October 2013. Over more than two years since then, we have together traveled an extraordinary journey that has taken us to the launch of the AIIB today.

In October 2014, the first group of 22 Prospective

Founding Members signed the Memorandum of Understanding on Establishing the AIIB. In June 2015, representatives from 50 Prospective Founding Members signed the Articles of Agreement of the Asian Infrastructure Investment Bank. Before the end of last year, seven other Prospective Founding Members left their signatures on the Agreement. In December 2015, the Agreement met the legal threshold for entry into force and the AIIB was thence officially founded.

We owe the above-mentioned progress and achievements to the strong dedication and collaboration of all AIIB members, who have impressed us with their open minds, their inclusiveness, their determination to seek practical results through common development, and their craving for professional excellence as seen in the high standard and efficient operation of the AIIB. Member states have demonstrated a strong cooperative spirit throughout the negotiation, policy-making and senior management selection processes. This has made it possible for us to reach early agreement on key issues regarding the AIIB. Member states were quick to complete the domestic signing and ratification process, thus allowing the Agreement to enter into force as scheduled. This testifies in full to the member states' commitment and support for the AIIB to come into being. In the course leading up to the founding of the AIIB, member states acted in strict compliance with multilateral procedures, making sure that the AIIB becomes a truly international, rule-based and high-standard institution in all aspects involving its governance structure, operation policy, safeguards and procurement policy, and human resources management.

The founding of the AIIB proves once again that whenever there is a will, there will be a way. We are confident that when faced with the task of advancing world peace and development, so long as the international community has the will to build consensus and make win-win progress, we will be able to draw the big plan, and also turn it into reality.

Ladies and gentlemen,

Dear friends,

The founding and opening of the AIIB will effectively boost investment to support infrastructure development in Asia. It will serve to channel more resources, particularly private investment, into infrastructure projects to promote regional connectivity and economic integration. It will usher in a better investment environment, create more job opportunities, and trigger greater medium- to long-term development potential on the part of developing members in Asia. This, in turn, will give impetus to economic growth in Asia and the wider world.

The founding and opening of the AIIB also means a great deal to the reform of the global economic governance system. It is consistent with the evolving trends in the global economy and will help make the global economic governance system more just, more equitable, and more effective.

It is our hope that member states will continue to work with one heart and one mind, actively pitch in, and get the functions of the AIIB up and running as soon as possible, so that the AIIB can grow fast, become strong, and add to the strength of multilateral development banks, thus contributing even more to global development.

Ladies and gentlemen,

Dear friends,

The AIIB will remain committed to open regionalism. This new institution and existing multilateral development banks may complement each other to build mutual strength. With its inherent advantages and unique features, the AIIB can make the current multilateral system more dynamic, and facilitate the common development of multilateral institutions. The AIIB can become a professional and efficient platform to promote infrastructure-related investment and financing for the benefit of all sides. And the AIIB has its role to play in raising the level of infrastructure financing and of economic and social development in the region.

The demand for infrastructure development in Asia is enormous. Institutions for infrastructure investment, old or new, have much to offer each other, and can work well together through joint financing, knowledge sharing, and capacity building. They may engage with each other in benign competition, learn from and reinforce each other, and move forward in parallel. This is a way to allow multilateral development institutions to contribute more to infrastructure connectivity and sustainable economic development in the region.

The AIIB should adapt itself to new trends in international

development and accommodate the diverse needs of developing members. It should explore new business models and financing tools, and help member states develop more infrastructure projects that are of higher quality and involve lower costs. While developing countries make up the mainstay of the AIIB membership, the institution has also attracted a large number of developed members. This unique strength makes it a bridge and a bond to facilitate both South-South cooperation and North-South cooperation.

The AIIB should function as a multilateral development bank as far as its operating model and principles are concerned. It should learn from the experience and best practices of existing multilateral development banks in terms of governance structure, social and environmental policies, procurement policy, and debt sustainability. Mutual learning and sharing helps the AIIB function according to high standards.

Ladies and gentlemen,

Dear friends,

China has taken an active part in, made a constructive contribution to, and benefited from the international development system. The initiative to establish the AIIB is a constructive move. It will enable China to take on more international responsibilities, improve the current international economic system, and provide more international public goods. This is a move that will help bring mutual benefits and win-win outcomes to all sides.

China, as the initiator of the AIIB, will firmly support its operation and development. In addition to subscribing capital according to plan, China will contribute US$50 million to the project preparation special fund to be established shortly, to support preparation for infrastructure development projects in less-developed member states.

The year 2016 is the first year of China's 13th Five-year Plan. China will aspire to achieve innovative, coordinated, green, open and inclusive development. The focus of agenda will be on promoting innovation-driven development to strengthen new drivers for economic development, on promoting supply-side structural reform to adapt to and lead the new normal of economic development, and on opening wider to the outside world with more emphasis given to advancing high-level and two-way opening up. China has the confidence and capability to ensure sustained and sound economic development and bring more opportunities and benefits to Asia and beyond.

China will continue to contribute to global development and will continue to pursue a mutually beneficial strategy of opening up. The door of China's opening up will never shut, and China welcomes all countries to board its development express. China stands ready to work with other parties to make sure that the AIIB will start to operate and play its due role as soon as possible, and contribute to economic growth and better lives for people in developing countries. And China continues to welcome the AIIB and other international financial institutions to take part in building the Silk Road Economic Belt and the 21st Century Maritime Silk Road.

Ladies and gentlemen,

Dear friends,

As the saying goes, the bonfire burns higher when everyone adds firewood. The AIIB belongs to all its member states. It is designed to facilitate common development in the region and the world at large. To succeed, it needs to count on the solidarity, cooperation and synergy of all sides.

I hope and believe that through the joint efforts of all member states, the AIIB will become a new multilateral development bank for the 21st century that is professional, efficient, and clean in operation. It will also be a new platform to help foster a global community of shared future, to make a new contribution to prosperity in Asia and beyond, and to lend new strength to improving global economic governance!

Thank you.

Comply with the Trend of Economic Globalization and Grow Stronger*

January 18, 2016

We should establish a new system of opening up.

China's development achievements over the past 30 years derive from opening up. The prosperity of a country and the rejuvenation of a nation mostly rely on following the trend of the times and propelling historical progress.

Economic globalization is the trend we have to recognize in planning our development. The concept of "economic globalization" became popular after the Cold War ended, but it is not a new phenomenon. As early as the 19th century, Karl Marx and Frederick Engels elaborated theories on world trade, world markets, and world history in *The German Ideology, Manifesto of the Communist Party, Economic Manuscript of 1857-1858, Capital* and other works. They pointed out in the *Manifesto of the Communist Party*: "The bourgeois has through its exploration of the world market given a cosmopolitan character to production and consumption in every country."

---

* Part of the speech at a study session on implementing the decisions of the Fifth Plenary Session of the 18th CPC Central Committee, attended by officials at the provincial/ministerial level.

Marx and Engels' perception and arguments revealed the nature, logic, and process of economic globalization, laying a theoretical foundation for us to understand the concept today.

Economic globalization underwent three general stages. First, colonial expansion and the formation of the world market. Western countries, through plunder, occupation by force, and colonial expansion, had largely completed the carve-up of the world before the outbreak of World War I, bringing all regions and nations into a single capitalist world system. Second, two parallel world markets. After World War II, a number of socialist countries emerged, and colonial and semi-colonial countries declared their independence, which divided the world into two camps and formed two parallel markets in the international economy. Third, economic globalization. As the Cold War ended in 1991, opposition between the two camps and the two parallel world markets disappeared; interdependence between countries increased; and economic globalization quickened its pace.

Accordingly, China's relationship with the world also underwent three stages.

First, from national seclusion to semi-colonialism and semi-feudalism. Before the Opium War, China was isolated from the world market and global industrialization. After that, during the wars against Western aggression, China suffered repeated defeats and fell to the status of a poor and weak country.

Second, sole alliance with the Soviet Union and national semi-seclusion, and then complete seclusion. After the founding of the PRC in 1949, China explored the path of building socialism in sole alliance with the Soviet Union and in semi-seclusion from the rest of the world, and almost completely separated itself from the international community during the Cultural Revolution.

Third, multi-dimensional opening up. Since reform and opening up in 1978, China has taken advantage of economic globalization and steadily opened ever-wider to the outside world, marking a historic change.

Practice has proved that to develop and grow stronger, we must comply with the trend of economic globalization, adhere to opening up, and make full use of advanced scientific achievements and management experience. During the early period of reform and opening up, when we lacked strength and experience, many people doubted whether we could benefit from reform and opening up without becoming corroded and being swallowed up by the dominant Western countries. In those years, we came under heavy pressure in pushing the negotiations on China's accession to the General Agreement on Tariffs and Trade and the World Trade Organization. Looking back today, we chose the correct direction of development by opening up the country and going global.

Twenty or even 15 years ago, the major propellants of economic globalization were the US and other Western countries. Today, China is considered the biggest driver of global trade liberalization and facilitation, resisting various forms of Western protectionism. This proves that as long as we consciously support the trend of global development, we can grow stronger and lead world development.

In promoting open development, the domestic and international situations we face now are quite different from the past. On the whole, we have more favorable factors; we also face significant risks and challenges that are by no means negligible. This can be seen from four perspectives.

First, power structures among various countries are changing positively in an unprecedented way. The rise of emerging market economies and developing countries is changing the global political and economic landscapes. There is an irresistible trend towards world polarization and democracy in international relations. The West-dominated global governance system is finally showing signs of change, but the competition to gain dominance in global governance and the formulation of international rules is fierce. Since Western developed countries retain advantages in economy, science and technology, politics, and military affairs, there is a long way to go to build a fairer and more equitable international political and economic order.

Second, the world economy is gradually emerging from the shadow of the global financial crisis. Western countries are maintaining the momentum of economic recovery through reindustrialization. The structure of the international industrial division of labor has changed, but protectionism remains severe worldwide. The formulation of international economic and trade rules tends to be politicized and fragmented. Emerging market economies and developing economies are still sluggish, and the global economy has not yet found new engines for full recovery.

Third, China's share of the world economy and global governance has increased rapidly. China is now the world's second largest economy, its largest exporter, its second largest importer, its second largest source of foreign direct investment, its largest holder of foreign exchange reserves, and its largest market for tourism. China has become a major factor in changing the world political and economic landscapes. Nevertheless, it remains the case that China's economy is big but not strong, and our per capita income and living standards are not in the same league as those of Western countries. We need to work harder to turn our economic strength into international institutional authority.

Fourth, China's opening up has reached a better balance between bringing in and going global. The opening-up pattern has changed from mainly bringing in to both bringing in and going global on a large scale, but the corresponding law, consultancy, finance, personnel, risk management, and safety controls cannot meet the practical needs, while our mechanisms remain weak in supporting high-level opening up and large-scale going global.

This means that the overall environment for open development is more favorable than ever before, but the conflicts, risks, and contests we are facing are also unprecedented, setting delicate traps for any potential negligence. On the subject of the next steps in open development, the Fifth Plenary Session of the 18th CPC Central Committee made pertinent provisions, and I also set out some requirements in the speech at the second full assembly. I hope we continue to explore and practice, enhance our conscientiousness and capabilities to address the overall situation both domestically and internationally, and improve the effectiveness and level of opening up.

Promote the Belt and Road Initiative, Extend Reform and Development*

April 29, 2016

The Belt and Road Initiative is an important measure in enabling China to implement all-round opening up, and a major platform for promoting mutual benefit in the current era. We should redouble our efforts to implement the initiative from a higher ground and a broader perspective, on the basis of rich historical experience, and equipped with innovative ideas and concepts, so that the initiative will truly benefit peoples of all countries along the routes.

The Political Bureau has chosen this topic for today's group study session to help us understand the history and culture of the overland Silk Road and the Maritime Silk Road, and learn from historical experience in order to further the Belt and Road Initiative. The initiative has attracted considerable attention from the international community. The reasons for this are that the initiative responds to the call of the times and meets the desire of countries for faster development, and that it has a profound historical origin and

---

* Main points of the speech at the 31st group study session of the Political Bureau of the 18th CPC Central Committee.

popular foundation. For our own part, the initiative meets our country's need for economic growth, and is conducive to the development of border regions mainly inhabited by ethnic minorities.

The initiative has evoked the historical memory of participating countries. The ancient Silk Road was more a route of friendship than a route of trade. In the course of friendly exchanges between the Chinese and other peoples along the route, a Silk Road spirit featuring peace, cooperation, openness, inclusiveness, mutual learning and mutual benefit has taken shape. We should inherit and carry forward the Silk Road spirit, combining China's development with that of other countries involved in the initiative, and the Chinese Dream with dreams of other peoples, and imbue it with new life.

To promote the initiative, we have to maintain a proper balance between the interests of our country and those of other countries, between the government, the market and society, between economic and trade cooperation and people-to-people exchanges, between opening up and national security, between implementation and publicity, and between national and local objectives.

China is the initiator and propeller of the Belt and Road Initiative, but the initiative is not China's business alone. Therefore, focusing on China's own development, it should also welcome other countries to board China's express train of development, and help them realize their own development objectives. We should pay greater attention to the interests of other countries while pursuing our own. We should stick to the sound values of upholding the greater good and pursuing shared interests, with high priority given to the greater good. We should not seek quick successes and instant benefits, nor should we engage in short-term behavior. We must adopt a holistic approach to the common interests of China and other countries and their respective interests and concerns. We must identify more areas for converging interests, and give full play to all participating countries. Our enterprises must give greater importance to their good reputation in their going-global activities, while seeking their investment returns. They must abide by laws of the recipient countries, and shoulder more social responsibilities.

To promote the initiative, we must give play to both the role of the government and that of the market. The government must play a leading role in promotion, coordination and building mechanisms. At the same time, it is important to put in place a market-based regional economic cooperation mechanism for enterprises. The government should encourage enterprises and other social forces to participate in the initiative, with a view to forming a cooperation model that features guidance by the government, participation of enterprises and support of people's organizations.

People-to-people and cultural exchanges are also an integral part of the initiative. To implement the initiative, we must create an atmosphere in which people of all participating countries appreciate, understand and respect each other. Closer people-to-people ties represent an important element of the initiative as well as a popular and cultural foundation. We must promote economic cooperation and cultural exchanges simultaneously. We must work meticulously in the field of cultural exchanges, respecting the culture, history, customs and lifestyles of all countries, and increase friendly exchanges with peoples of the participating countries, so as to lay a good social foundation for the development of the initiative. We must enhance cooperation in the field of security, endeavor to build a community of shared interests, shared responsibility and shared future, and foster a favorable environment. We should direct our attention to promotional efforts and make them effective, try all means to explain and carry across the message of the initiative, and cultivate a good environment of public opinion in support of the initiative.

The implementation of the initiative requires both the overall objective of the state and local enthusiasm. Local planning and objectives should conform to the national objective and serve the overall interests. We should focus on opening wider to the outside world, enhancing our ability to participate in international competition, transforming the growth model, and restructuring the economy. We must base ourselves on local reality, identify and give play to the role of local governments, make practical progress, and expand the space for reform and development.

Belt and Road Development Is the Joint Cause of All Countries Along the Routes[*]

June 20, 2016

Jointly building the Belt and Road through consultation, promoting regional economic prosperity, and safeguarding world peace and stability conform with the requirements of the times and comply with the common aspirations of the people. The Silk Road spirit should be carried forward so that we can create and enjoy a bright future.

Since the Belt and Road Initiative was proposed three years ago, it has been warmly welcomed by countries along the routes and made self-evident progress. This shows that the spirit of mutual learning and mutual benefit holds sway, and faith in peace, cooperation, openness and inclusiveness now stretches long and unbroken over thousands of miles. As the countries along the routes differ in culture, national conditions, and stage of development, it is important to respect each other while working together, coexist with our differences, help the poor and the disadvantaged,

---

[*] Main points of the speech, titled "Join Hands to Create a Better Future", at the opening ceremony of the Silk Road Forum and China-Poland Regional Cooperation and Business Forum in Warsaw.

and develop in a balanced manner. The Belt and Road development is the joint cause of countries along the routes, which requires joint efforts to cooperate, develop and share.

The Polish people are good friends and partners of the Chinese, and Poland and China have enjoyed a long-term friendship. Both sides are willing to work for the prosperity of the BRI region, and play a greater role in regional cooperation. I would like to put forward five suggestions on the Belt and Road development, cooperation between China and Central and Eastern European countries (CEEC), and China-Poland cooperation.

First, we should make concerted efforts to establish China-Poland cooperation as a model of Belt and Road cooperation, so as to drive forward overall regional cooperation.

Second, we should highlight key areas and give priority to economic and trade cooperation. Both sides should jointly push forward the establishment of China-EU trade and investment mechanisms, liberalize and facilitate trade and investment, and integrate Europe's strengths in advanced technology, China's strengths in manufacturing, and Poland's strengths in location and human resources to create a new trade center and economic growth pole.

Third, we should cooperate closely to coordinate China-CEEC cooperation with the Belt and Road Initiative, so as to build long-lasting and practical China-CEEC ties.

Fourth, we should improve the mechanism to forge a synergy of local governments, enterprises and other NGOs. Local governments of China and Poland should continue to strengthen communication, and better connect local enterprises and other NGOs of the two countries, so as to expand practical cooperation in all fields and consolidate the public foundations of Poland-China friendship.

Fifth, we should prioritize and strengthen the leading and supporting role of think tanks. Research on the development plans and the routes of the Belt and Road should be intensified to advise and assist governments in planning connectivity, policy coordination and mechanism design, and think tanks should act as a bridge for communicating ideas, interpreting policies and channeling public opinion.

China has confidence in its ability to maintain medium-to-high speed economic growth, and welcomes other countries to board the China's express train of development. We should join hands, cooperate with sincerity, and carry forward the Silk Road spirit, so as to build a community of shared interests, shared responsibility and shared future at an early date and jointly create and enjoy bright prospects.

Jointly Build China-Central Asia-West Asia Economic Corridor*

June 22, 2016

The Silk Road Economic Belt, a proposal I made during my 2013 visit to Central Asia, won wide support and an active response from the international community, including Uzbekistan. Later I also proposed the idea of the 21st Century Maritime Silk Road.

The Silk Road is a great treasure of history. Inspired by the legacy of the ancient network of trade routes, the Belt and Road Initiative aspires to humanity's common dream of peace and development, and offers the world a solution for common prosperity and development grounded in Eastern wisdom.

For three years the Belt and Road Initiative has grown amid experiments and cooperation, and improved along the way. Based on extensive consultation, joint contribution and shared benefits, we strive to build a community of shared future and interests, and have won the wide recognition of

---

* Part of the speech, titled "Working Together for New Glories of the Silk Road", made at the Legislative Chamber of the Supreme Assembly of Uzbekistan.

participating countries under the guidance of peace and co-operation, openness and inclusiveness, mutual learning, and mutual benefit. To date more than 70 countries and international organizations have taken part in the Belt and Road Initiative. China has released the Vision and Actions on Jointly Building Silk Road Economic Belt and 21st Century Maritime Silk Road, and has signed BRI cooperation agreements with more than 30 countries. As more and more friends are joining in this endeavor, the Belt and Road Initiative is becoming a shared goal of all peoples along the routes.

During my last visit President Islam Karimov shared with me a saying in Uzbekistan: "An empty bag cannot stand erect." For the past three years the BRI countries have made continued efforts to coordinate policies, connect infrastructure networks, facilitate trade and capital flows, and strengthen people-to-people ties, with deeper cooperation and notable progress in many areas. China has put pen to paper on industrial cooperation deals with 20 countries and jointly set up 46 overseas economic cooperation zones in 17 Belt and Road countries, with accumulated Chinese investment topping US$14 billion and creating 60,000 local jobs. The AIIB went into operation with 57 participating countries, along with the establishment of the Silk Road Fund and the China-Eurasian Economic Cooperation Fund. Each year, China funds 10,000 students from Belt and Road countries to study in China. In 2015 China's trade with countries participating in the Belt and Road Initiative surpassed US$1 trillion, accounting for a quarter of its total foreign trade. Chinese enterprises' direct investment in 49 countries along the routes reached nearly US$15 billion in 2015, up 18 percent year on year, while Belt and Road countries' investment in China exceeded US$8.2 billion, up 25 percent year on year. As its initial planning and configuration have been completed, the Belt and Road Initiative is now stepping into the stage of full implementation of agreed projects and sustained development.

Taken together, the large markets and abundant resources of Belt and Road countries and their strong mutual complementarity offer huge potential and development prospects. "A good plan needs good timing to work," said an ancient Chinese philosopher. China is willing to work with Uzbekistan and all sides to grasp historic opportunities, address risks and challenges, and promote the Belt and Road Initiative in both breadth and depth.

First, build a cooperation network for mutual benefit. China will work with Belt and Road countries, follow the trend of the times, and carry on the spirit of the Silk Road, in an effort to strengthen trust, consolidate friendship, deepen cooperation, and increase mutual support. On the basis of the principles of voluntariness, equality and mutual benefit, we will join hands to build a win-win cooperation network for the Belt and Road Initiative featuring pragmatism, enterprise, inclusiveness, mutual learning, openness, innovation and common development, and contribute to the revitalization of the global economy.

Second, pioneer a new model of cooperation. China upholds the principle of extensive consultation, joint contribution and shared benefits, and synergizes development plans among countries joining in the Belt and Road Initiative. On that basis, China will carry out bilateral and regional cooperation and create a new cooperation model underpinned by liberalizing and facilitating trade and investment, focusing on connectivity, industrial cooperation and people-to-people exchanges, and enabled by mutually beneficial financial cooperation. China will continue to increase input and provide all-dimensional support for the initiative, so as to benefit all participants.

Third, build a multi-layer cooperation platform. China will work with partner countries to develop a new multi-player, all-dimensional and cross-sectoral platform of win-win cooperation. China will promote mutually beneficial cooperation among governments, enterprises, social institutions, and NGOs. Enterprises and private capital are especially encouraged to take part.

Fourth, drive projects in key areas. China will work with partner countries to build six major international economic corridors, establish more industrial clusters and economic and trade cooperation zones, and encourage cooperation in key areas. Together with its partner countries, China will continue to improve infrastructure networks, decide on a number of connectivity projects that will boost regional cooperation, and discuss cross-border cooperation on customs clearance. China will press forward with international industrial cooperation, continue to provide the world with high-quality and environmentally friendly industry and advanced technology and equipment, and help partner countries improve their industrial structure and enhance their level of industrialization. China will develop new ways for financial cooperation, expand the scale and scope of local currency settlement with partner countries, and develop offshore Renminbi business and financial products in Belt and Road countries. China will strengthen cooperation with partner countries in the fields of education, science and technology, culture, sports, tourism, health and archeology, set up a big data exchange platform, and build a cooperation network of BRI think tanks.

Priority will be given to deeper cooperation in environmental protection, green development, ecological conservation, and therefore a "green Silk Road". In building a Silk Road for health promotion, China will strive to expand cooperation in medical care and health in such fields as the alert of communicable diseases, disease prevention and control, medical assistance and traditional medicine. On human resources cooperation, China proposed a vocational skills alliance to train and produce professionals in various fields. On the security front, China calls for fostering a governance model with Asian features and upholding common, comprehensive, cooperative and sustainable security in Asia, and building a Silk Road for peace.

Central Asia was a key region along the ancient Silk Road. For three years Central Asian countries have actively joined the BRI effort, achieving a series of important early wins and setting a good example. With strengths passed down through history, in geographical proximity, cultural bonds and political and legal support, the Belt and Road Initiative has won wide support from the people of Central Asia. China sees Central Asia as a key area and an important partner in BRI cooperation. Both sides should make greater efforts to coordinate their development strategies and plans, explore broader areas of cooperation, and increase the level of cooperation. We are willing to work with Central Asian countries in building the China-Central Asia-West Asia Economic Corridor.

China will host a Belt and Road Forum for International Cooperation in 2017. It is my hope that this forum will serve as a platform for our partner countries to communicate, pool ideas, and build consensus on the Belt and Road Initiative.

The Belt and Road Initiative
Benefits the People*

August 17, 2016

We must review the experience gained and advance the Belt and Road Initiative with full confidence, focusing on policy coordination, connectivity of infrastructure, unimpeded trade, financial integration and closer people-to-people ties, highlighting the establishment of mutually beneficial and cooperative networks, new modes of cooperation, and multilateral cooperation platforms, and joining hands to build a road of green development, of health cooperation, of innovation and of peace. Like driving a nail with a hammer, we should push the initiative forward step by step to ensure peoples along the routes benefit from the initiative.

Since the 18th CPC National Congress in 2012, the Central Committee has identified, with an eye to development as planned for the 13th Five-year Plan period (2016-2020) and longer term, three major development strategies: the Belt and Road Initiative, the Coordinated Development of Beijing, Tianjin and Hebei, and the Yangtze River Eco-

---

* Main points of the speech at a conference on the Belt and Road Initiative.

nomic Belt. In 2014 we approved the Strategic Planning for the Building of the Silk Road Economic Belt and the 21st Century Maritime Silk Road. In 2015 we released the Vision and Actions on Jointly Building Silk Road Economic Belt and 21st Century Maritime Silk Road, which is to be complemented by local and departmental plans and which has attracted international attention.

At present, more than 100 countries and international organizations have joined the initiative. China has signed cooperation agreements on building the Belt and Road with more than 30 countries, and entered into international industrial cooperation with more than 20 countries. The United Nations and other international organizations have also positively responded to the initiative. There has been further financial cooperation involving the Asian Infrastructure Investment Bank (AIIB), the Silk Road Fund and others, and a number of influential landmark projects have been implemented. The initiative started from scratch, but is now progressing rapidly, yielding rich results beyond expectation.

Only a strong and prosperous country can open itself to the outside world with confidence, and openness in turn promotes further prosperity. China's achievements since the beginning of reform and opening up in 1978 have proved that openness is an important driver of its economic and social development. As China becomes the world's second largest economy and its economy enters the new normal, to maintain sustainable and healthy economic growth we must have a global vision, take a holistic approach to the situation both at home and abroad, and develop a grand and comprehensive opening-up strategy. We must embrace the world in a more proactive manner.

We will take advantage of the initiative to increase transnational connections and communications, and enhance cooperation in trade and investment, and in industry and equipment manufacturing. What is essential is to rebalance the world economy by fostering new demand and ensuring effective supply. Particularly in the current situation where the world economy has remained sluggish, it will help to stabilize the world economy if procyclical industrial and building capacity could be used by participating countries to meet the pressing demand for industrialization, modernization and infrastructure.

To promote the Belt and Road Initiative, first we must build up consensus. We should, through joint planning and shared development for mutual benefit, focus on key regions, countries and projects, concentrate on development, and strive to benefit not only the people of China but also — and more importantly – people from other countries along the routes. China welcomes others on board its express train of development. All other countries and international organizations are welcome to join the initiative.

Second, we should ensure well-organized implementation of our plans, and work out measures and policies to promote the initiative. We should focus on innovation, improve supporting services, and give priority to such projects of strategic importance as the connectivity of infrastructure, the development and utilization of energy, the building of economic, trade and industrial cooperation zones, and the research and development of core industrial technologies.

Third, we should promote a coordinated and balanced development, between land and sea, between China and foreign countries, and between governments and enterprises. We will encourage Chinese enterprises to invest in other countries along the routes, which are also welcome to invest in China. We will strengthen the complementarity between the initiative and national strategies, including the Coordinated Development of Beijing, Tianjin and Hebei, and the Yangtze River Economic Belt. To take a holistic and integrated approach to the initiative on the one hand and other programs on the other, such as the development of west China, the revitalization of northeast China, the rise of central China, the earlier start of east China and the development and opening up of the border regions, we will be able to achieve all-round opening up and integrated development of east, central, and west China.

Fourth, we should launch key projects first. We may start with a few demonstration projects for early harvest, in particular, projects for infrastructure connectivity, cooperation in industrial capacity, and trade and industrial cooperation zones, so that countries involved will have a true sense of achievement.

Fifth, we should promote financial innovation to facilitate the initiative, creating innovative international financing models, expanding financial cooperation, building multilevel financial platforms, and establishing a financial security system that is enduring, stable, and sustainable, and keeps risks under control.

Sixth, we should foster close people-to-people ties, carry forward the Silk Road spirit, and promote cultural exchanges and mutual learning.

Seventh, we should enhance publicity on the achievements of the initiative and increase academic research, theoretical support, and channels for communications.

Eighth, we should strengthen security, improving risk assessment, monitoring, early warning, and emergency response. We should establish a sound working mechanism and define the implementation steps, so as to ensure that all departments, project management units or enterprises that are involved properly follow the arrangements and measures.

A New Starting Point for China's Development, A New Blueprint for Global Growth[*]

September 3, 2016

Ladies and gentlemen,

Dear friends,

Good afternoon! I am so glad to have all of you with us here in Hangzhou. The G20 Summit will begin tomorrow, an event much anticipated by the international community as well as by the business community, by think tanks, and by labor, women and youth organizations. And all of us share one and the same goal – that is, to make the Hangzhou Summit deliver fruitful outcomes.

Hangzhou is a renowned historical and cultural city and a center of business and trade in China. Famous for Bai Juyi and Su Dongpo, as well as for the West Lake and the Grand Canal, Hangzhou has a fascinating history and rich and enchanting cultural heritage. Hangzhou is also an innovative and vibrant city with booming e-commerce. One click of a mouse in Hangzhou, and you can connect to the whole world. Hangzhou is also a leader in ecological conservation.

---

* Keynote speech at the opening ceremony of the B20 Summit in Hangzhou, China.

159

Its green hills and clear lakes and rivers delight the eye on sunny days and present a distinctive view on rainy days. Hangzhou is imbued with a charm unique to the south of the Yangtze River that has been fostered over many generations.

I spent six years working in Zhejiang Province and was personally involved in its development. So I am familiar with everything here, with its land and its people. In China, there are many cities like Hangzhou which have gone through great changes and achieved tremendous development over the decades. Millions of ordinary Chinese families have changed their lives through hard work. When added up, these small changes have become a powerful force driving China's development and progress. What we see here in Hangzhou showcases what has been achieved in the great course of China's reform and opening up.

– This is a course of blazing a new trail. Modernizing an enormous country with a population of more than 1.3 billion is an endeavor never before undertaken in the history of mankind, and this means China must pursue its own path of development. There is a Chinese saying that expresses what we have done: "crossing the river by feeling for stones." We have driven reform and opening up to a deeper level, broken new ground, forged ahead, and established and developed socialism with distinctive Chinese features.

– This is a course of delivering tangible outcomes. We have pursued economic development as the top priority and never slackened our efforts. We have moved with the times and taken bold initiatives. Thanks to our perseverance, resolve, and dedication, and to the spirit of "driving the nail", we have succeeded in turning China into the world's second biggest economy, the biggest trader of goods, and the third largest direct overseas investor, and we have lifted China's per capita GDP to close to 8,000 US dollars.

– This is a course of achieving common prosperity. Development is for the people; it should be pursued by the people and its outcomes should be shared by the people. This is what China's reform, opening up, and drive for socialist modernization are all about. Thanks to this reform and opening up, China has lifted more than 700 million people out of poverty and made significant improvements to the lives of more than 1.3 billion people. In pursuing development, we have accomplished in just a few decades what has taken other countries several hundred years to achieve.

– This is a course of China and the world embracing each other. We have pursued an independent foreign policy of peace and a fundamental policy of opening up. We have endeavored to develop in an open environment, starting by introducing large-scale overseas investment and then reciprocating by striding forth into the wider world. We have been actively involved in building a fairer and more equitable international order. China's interactions with the outside world have deepened. And indeed, we have friends all over the world.

Ladies and gentlemen,

Dear friends,

Thirty-eight years of reform and opening up have unfolded

rapidly. Today, as China's economy grows in size and its co-operation with the world expands, the prospects for China's economy have drawn keen international attention. Many people ponder whether China can maintain sustainable and steady growth, whether China can continue its reform and opening up, and whether China can avoid falling into the "middle income trap".

Actions speak louder than words – and China has answered these questions with actions. Early this year, China drew up the outlines of the 13th Five-year Plan for economic and social development. These outlines call for implementing a vision of innovative, coordinated, green, open and inclusive development, addressing acute challenges of uneven, uncoordinated and unsustainable development, and ultimately achieving a moderately prosperous society in all respects.

China has reached a new historical starting point. It is a new starting point for China to deepen reform across the board and foster new drivers of economic and social development. It is a new starting point for China to adapt its economy to a new normal and transform its growth model. It is a new starting point for China to further integrate itself into the world and open itself wider to the world. We are confident in our ability to maintain a medium-to-high rate of growth and deliver more development opportunities to the world, while ensuring our own development.

– Proceeding from this new starting point, we will resolutely strive for deeper all-round reform and open up brighter prospects of development. China's economic development has entered a new normal, a stage it cannot bypass if China is to upgrade its economy and achieve a better structure. Reform is crucial to maintaining a medium-to-high rate of growth under the new normal. Sticking to conventional thinking will get us nowhere. Fearing to advance will only result in losing the opportunity. China's goal of reform has been set and we will not deviate from it. China will take sure and firm steps in advancing reform and will not slow down its pace.

China's reform has left the foothills and entered the mountains, where tough challenges must be met. We have the resolve to make painful self-adjustments and tackle problems that have built up over many years – particularly underlying issues and entrenched interests – and carry reform through to the end. We will continue to carry out supply-side structural reform, resolve major problems in economic development, and improve the performance of the supply system by optimizing factors allocation and adjusting industrial structure. Through these efforts, we can energize the market and achieve coordinated development. We will continue to explore new institutional mechanisms, break through the resistance of vested interests, exercise law-based governance, and better leverage both the decisive role of the market in resource allocation and the role of the government.

– Proceeding from the new starting point, we will pursue an innovation-driven development strategy to create stronger growth drivers. Scientific and technological innovation holds the key to development. We are keenly aware that in spite of their scale, many sectors of China's economy are not strong enough or competitive enough. Over the years, they have depended on input of resources, capital, and labor to achieve growth and expand scale. But this model is no longer sustainable. China now faces the challenging task of changing its growth drivers and growth model and adjusting its economic structure. To make China an innovative country and a leader in science and technology is what we must now do in pursuing development.

We are implementing the innovation-driven development strategy so as to leverage the role of innovation as the primary growth driver and make growth quality-based rather than quantity-based. We will promote omni-dimensional, multi-tiered and wide-ranging changes in principles guiding development, institutional structures, and business models so as to bring about a fundamental transformation of the forces driving development and give it new impetus. We will strive to make breakthroughs in major projects and priority areas and take the lead in undertaking major international scientific programs and projects. We will conduct research on, and find solutions to pressing scientific and technological issues holding back economic and industrial development. We will speed up the commercialization of R&D successes to meet the need of shifting the growth model, adjusting the economic structure, building a modern industrial system, fostering strategic emerging industries, and developing a modern service industry. In short, we aim to move our industries and products towards the medium-high end of the value chain and create more innovation-driven growth areas with first-mover advantages that will lead development.

– Proceeding from the new starting point, we will promote green development to achieve better economic performance. I have said many times that green mountains and clear water are as good as mountains of gold and silver. To protect the environment is to protect productivity, and to improve the environment is to boost productivity. This simple fact is winning increased public recognition.

We will unwaveringly pursue a strategy of sustainable development and stay committed to green, low-carbon and circular development and China's fundamental policy of conserving resources and protecting the environment. In promoting green development, we also aim to address climate change and overcapacity. In the next five years, China's water consumption, energy consumption, and CO_2 emissions per unit of GDP will be cut down by 23, 15 and 18 percent respectively. We will make China a beautiful country with blue sky, green vegetation and clear rivers, so that the people will enjoy life in an attractive environment with the ecological benefits created by economic development.

As from 2016, we are vigorously advancing supply-side structural reform and adjusting the relationship between supply and demand. We will cut down production capacity of crude steel by another 100 to 150 million tons in the next five years, and close coal mines with production capacity of around 500 million tons, and cut production capacity of around 500 million tons through coal mine restructuring in three to five years. This is an initiative that we are taking to cut excess capacity, adjust the economic structure and pursue steady growth so as to sustain long-term development. China has taken the most robust and solid measures in cutting excess capacity and we will honor our commitment with actions.

– Proceeding from the new starting point, we will promote equity and sharing of development outcomes to deliver more benefits to the people. "The people are the foundation of a country, and only when the people lead a good life can the country thrive." We need to be people-oriented, a principle that we should follow in everything we do in advancing economic and social development.

We will meet the people's aspirations for a better life, raise their living standards and the quality of their lives, improve the public services system and enlarge the middle-income group. In particular, we will provide stronger and more targeted support to those living in difficulty, so that those 57 million rural people living below the current poverty line will all be lifted out of poverty and poverty will be alleviated in all poor counties by 2020. Since the beginning of reform and opening up China has lifted more than 700 million people out of poverty – over 70 percent of the global population living in poverty – thus making a significant contribution to poverty reduction worldwide. And we will continue to contribute to the global fight against poverty. With more attention paid to equality and fairness, we will make the pie bigger and ensure that people get a fair share of it. We will resolve the most pressing problems affecting the immediate interests of the people to their satisfaction.

– Proceeding from the new starting point, we will open up wider to achieve greater mutual benefit and win-win outcomes. To pursue a win-win strategy and open up China in a more comprehensive, profound and diversified way is our strategic choice. China's opening up will not stall, still less will it reverse course.

We will continue to be fully involved in economic globalization and support the multilateral trading regime. We will expand access for foreign investment, facilitate such investment to promote fair and open competition, and create a sound business environment. We will also accelerate negotiation on FTAs and investment treaties with a range of countries and the development of high-standard pilot free trade zones in China. While carrying out market-based reform of the Renminbi exchange rate in an orderly manner and phasing in the opening of domestic capital market, we will continue efforts to make the Renminbi an international currency and further internationalize China's financial sector.

China's development has benefited from the international community, and we are ready to provide more public goods to the international community. I have proposed the initiative of building the Silk Road Economic Belt and the 21st Century Maritime Silk Road to share China's development opportunities with countries along the Belt and Road and achieve common prosperity. Major progress has been made in launching key projects and building the economic corridors of the Silk Road Economic Belt, and the building of the 21st Century Maritime Silk Road is well underway.

The Asian Infrastructure Investment Bank initiated by China has already started its positive role in regional infrastructure development.

Here, I wish to stress that the new mechanisms and initiatives launched by China are not intended to reinvent the wheel or target any other country. Rather, they aim to complement and improve existing international mechanisms to achieve win-win cooperation and common development. China's opening drive is not a one-man show. Rather, it is an invitation open to all. It is an initiative not intended to establish China's own sphere of influence, but to support common development of all countries. It is not meant to build a backyard garden for China, but a garden shared by all countries.

We are firm in our resolve to implement the abovementioned reform and development measures; and they have indeed worked. In the first half of this year China's GDP grew by 6.7 percent. Its industrial upgrading and structural adjustment picked up pace, final consumption expenditure contributed 73.4 percent to GDP, and the added value of the tertiary industry made up 54.1 percent of GDP. Household incomes grew steadily, and 7.17 million urban jobs were created. We have reasons to believe that China will embrace even better prospects and make a still greater contribution to the world.

Ladies and gentlemen,

Dear friends,

The world economy is now in a period of profound adjustment; it is following an erratic path to recovery. It stands at a crucial juncture where new growth drivers are taking the place of old ones. The dynamism provided by the last round of scientific and industrial revolution is waning, while new impetus for growth is still in the making. Currently, protectionism is rising. Global trade and investment are sluggish. The multilateral trading regime faces obstacles in development, and the emergence of various regional trade arrangements have led to fragmentation of rules. Complex geopolitical factors and regional flashpoints, as well as global challenges such as political and security conflicts and turmoil, the refugee crisis, climate change and terrorism, have all affected the world economy with consequences that cannot be overlooked.

Against such a complex background and in the context of the risks and challenges facing the world economy, the international community has placed high expectations on the G20 and the Hangzhou Summit. At the G20 Antalya Summit last year, I proposed that we make an accurate assessment of the health of the world economy and seek the right prescriptions for its ailments. China will work with other parties to ensure that the Hangzhou Summit comes up with an integrated prescription to address both symptoms and root causes, so that the world economy can move along a path of strong, sustainable, balanced and inclusive growth.

First, we need to build an innovative world economy to generate new drivers of growth. Innovation holds the key to unleashing fundamental growth potential. The new round of scientific and industrial revolution with the internet at its core is gathering momentum, and new technologies such as artificial intelligence and virtual reality are developing in leaps and bounds. The combination of the virtual economy and the real economy will bring revolutionary changes to our way of work and way of life. Such changes will not take place overnight or come problem-free. They require all countries to work together to maximize and accelerate their positive effects, while minimizing any potential negative impacts.

China has made "breaking a new path for growth" one of the major agenda items of the Hangzhou Summit and has worked for the formulation of a G20 Blueprint on Innovative Growth. What we want to achieve is impetus through innovation and vitality through reform. We need to seize the historic opportunity presented by innovation, the new scientific and technological revolution, industrial transformation and the digital economy to increase the medium- and long-term growth potential of the world economy. This will be the first time that the G20 has taken action on innovation. It is important for us to pool together the strengths of innovation-oriented policies from individual countries, and make sure that our action is guided with conceptual consensus and implemented according to concrete action plans with the required institutional guarantees. In light of the pronounced issue of lackluster global economic growth, we need to adopt innovative macro-economic policies and effectively combine fiscal and monetary policies with structural reform policies.

Second, we need to build an open world economy to expand the scope of development. The path of world economic development shows that inclusion brings progress and isolation leads to retrogression. To repeat the beggar-thy-neighbor approach will not help any country emerge from crisis or recession. It only narrows the space for common development in the world economy and will lead to a "lose-lose" scenario.

According to the teaching of Chinese classics, "The governance of a country should be based on simple customs procedures, improved infrastructure, convenience for business transactions, and preferential agricultural policies." What this implies is the importance of building an open world economy. China has put trade and investment high on the G20 agenda. We support the efforts of the G20 as it endeavors to strengthen institution-building in trade and investment, formulate a strategy for global trade growth and the guiding principles for global investment policy-making, consolidate the multilateral trading regime, and reaffirm its commitment against protectionism. We hope that these measures will open up broader markets and provide scope for the development of individual countries, and help revitalize trade and investment – the two major engines of growth.

Third, we need to build an interconnected world economy to forge interactive synergy. In the age of economic globalization, countries are closely linked in their development and they all rise and fall together. No country can seek development on its own; the one sure path is through coordination and cooperation. We need to realize interconnected development by revitalizing the world economy.

We need to increase the interconnection of our rules and policies. We need to maximize positive spillovers and minimize negative external impacts through coordination of our macro-economic policies. At the same time, we need to encourage mutual learning to address asymmetries in systems, policies and standards. We need to enhance the interconnection of our infrastructure. China has proposed the global infrastructure connectivity alliance initiative. We want to encourage multilateral development banks to adopt joint declaration of aspirations and give greater funds and intellectual support to infrastructure projects. The aim is to speed up the process of global infrastructure connectivity. We need to promote win-win interconnection, foster and improve the global value chain, and increase the participation of parties concerned so as to create a chain of win-win global growth.

Fourth, we need to build an inclusive world economy to strengthen the foundation for win-win outcomes. We need to eradicate poverty and hunger, and advance inclusive and sustainable development. This is not simply a moral responsibility that bears on the international community. It is an opportunity to unleash immeasurable effective demand. The world's Gini coefficient has reached around 0.7, higher than the recognized alarm level which stands at 0.6. This is an issue that demands our immediate attention. Meanwhile, global industrial restructuring has had its impact on different industries and communities. We need to face this issue squarely and handle it properly in order to make economic globalization more inclusive.

To realize the above goals, this year's G20 has, for the first time, put the issue of development front and center of the global macro-policy framework. The first action plan has been formulated for implementing the 2030 Agenda for Sustainable Development, and for the first time coordinated actions will support African countries and LDCs in their industrialization. All these are moves of pioneering significance. The parties have all committed themselves to working for the early entry into force of the Paris Agreement on climate change. We have also formulated joint action plans on energy accessibility, energy efficiency, renewable energy, and entrepreneurship, and we have strengthened cooperation on food security and agriculture. Our concerns are for the needs of different social strata and communities, especially the disadvantaged, and we encourage discussions among the countries concerned on public administration and improved redistribution policies.

We hope to convey a message to the international community that the G20 works for the interests not only of its 20 members, but of the whole world. We will work to ensure that growth and development benefit all countries and peoples and that the lives of all people, especially those in developing countries, will get better day by day.

Ladies and gentlemen,

Dear friends,

One action counts more than a dozen programs. I believe the G20 members should join the other members of the international community and act immediately and in good faith on the following:

First, we can work together to build a peaceful and stable international environment. History has proven time and again that without peace, there will be no development and without stability, there will be no prosperity. Countries are all closely linked in their security. No country can develop solely on its own or resolve all problems without working with others. It is important to reject the outdated Cold War mentality and build a new concept of common, comprehensive, cooperative and sustainable security. We call on all countries to cherish our hard-won peace and tranquility, and to play a constructive role in maintaining global and regional stability. All countries should uphold the purposes and principles of the UN Charter, adhere to multilateralism, settle disagreements and disputes through dialogue and consultation, seek consensus, and dissolve tensions. Let us make the international order more just and equitable.

The pursuit of harmony and coexistence has been part of the genetic makeup of the Chinese nation throughout history. It represents the very essence of Eastern civilization. China is committed to the path of peaceful development. The logic that a strong country is bound to seek hegemony no longer applies and the willful use of force will lead us nowhere. China is the biggest contributor of peacekeepers among the permanent members of the UN Security Council. The proud sons of the Chinese people are among the UN peacekeepers who gave their lives to the missions of peace in Mali and South Sudan not long ago. China will continue to fulfill its international obligations and serve as the builder and defender of world peace.

Second, we can work together to build a global partnership for win-win cooperation. In the era of economic globalization, there is no island completely cut off from the rest of the world. As members of the global village, we need to cultivate the awareness of a global community of shared future. Partnership is the most valuable asset of the G20, and the solution for all countries as they rise up together to meet global challenges.

We need to seek common ground while narrowing or shelving differences in an effort to build a new model of international relations featuring win-win cooperation. All countries, big or small, strong or weak, rich or poor, must treat each other as equals. We need to help each other achieve sound development as we work to ensure our own development. The world will be a better place only when everyone is better off.

We need to step up communication and coordination on major global issues and provide more public goods for the fostering of a peaceful, stable and prosperous world. We need to institute and steadily improve macro-economic policy coordination mechanisms and be mindful of the related and chain effects of our domestic policies, in order to ensure their positive rather than negative spillovers. We need to rely on partnerships, uphold the vision of win-win results, step up practical cooperation across the board, continue to enrich and expand cooperation, and ensure that such cooperation delivers outcomes to meet people's expectations. We need to enable people of different countries, cultures and historical backgrounds to deepen exchanges, enhance mutual understanding, and jointly build a global community of shared future.

Third, we can work together to improve global economic governance. As a Chinese saying goes, small-minded people attend to trivial matters while those with greater wisdom attend to the governance of institutions. As the world economic situation changes, it is necessary that global economic governance remains relevant and adaptive to the changing times. Global economic governance should be based on equality. It must better reflect the new realities of the world economic landscape, increase the representation and voice of emerging markets and developing countries, and ensure that all countries have equal rights, equal opportunities, and equal rules to follow in international economic cooperation.

Global economic governance should embrace openness. It should be based on open concepts, open policies, and open mechanisms so as to adapt to the changing situation. It should be open to constructive suggestions and the recommendations and aspirations of different quarters of society. It should encourage the active participation and integration of various parties, reject exclusive arrangements, and avoid closed governance mechanisms and fragmentation of rules. Global economic governance should be driven by cooperation, as global challenges require global responses, and cooperation is the required choice. Countries need to step up communication and coordination, accommodate each other's interests and concerns, and work together to discuss rules, build mechanisms, and meet challenges. Global economic governance should be a mechanism of sharing. It should be about participation by all and benefits for all. Instead of seeking dominance or winner-takes-all results, it should encourage the pooling of interests and win-win prospects.

At this stage, global economic governance should focus on the following:

• jointly ensuring equitable and efficient global financial governance and upholding the overall stability of the world economy;

• jointly fostering open and transparent global trade and investment governance to cement the multilateral trading regime and unleash the potential of global cooperation in economy, trade and investment;

• jointly establishing green and low-carbon global energy governance to promote global green development cooperation;

• jointly facilitating an inclusive and interconnected global development governance to implement the UN 2030 Agenda for Sustainable Development;

• jointly advancing the wellbeing of mankind.

The G20 has convened 10 summits; it has now come to a crucial juncture of development. One of the goals of China's G20 Presidency is to enable the G20 to transform from a crisis response mechanism focusing on short-term policies to one of long-term governance that shapes medium- to long-term policies, and to solidify its role as the premier forum for international economic governance.

Ladies and gentlemen,

Dear friends,

The business community is the main driver of growth. By convening the B20 Summit on the eve of the G20 Summit, China wishes to pool all the ideas and wisdom of the business community. I am pleased to see that business representatives from the G20 countries have taken an active part in the G20 process throughout the year. Together with representatives of other communities, you have presented your views and suggestions on financing growth, on trade and investment, infrastructure, SME development, employment, and anti-corruption, and on other priority issues of the G20. You have provided important recommendations for G20 policy-making and contributed positively to the Hangzhou Summit.

Ladies and gentlemen,

Dear friends,

The tidal bore is currently sweeping up the Qiantang River. As an ancient Chinese poem reads, "The tide riders surf the currents; the flags they hold up never get wet." I, like all of you, look forward to a G20 that will ride the tides of the world economy. I believe that with various parties working together, the Hangzhou Summit is certain to achieve success.

In conclusion, I wish the B20 Summit a full success.

Thank you.

Build an Innovative, Invigorated, Interconnected, and Inclusive World Economy[*]

September 4, 2016

Dear colleagues,

I declare the G20 Hangzhou Summit open.

I am pleased to meet you all here in Hangzhou. First of all, I want to extend a warm welcome to you.

Last year's G20 Antalya Summit was a great success, and I want to take this opportunity to thank Turkey, which chaired last year's summit, again for its outstanding job and for achieving positive results. Turkey made "strong, sustainable and balanced growth through collective action" the theme of the summit, and promoted results in terms of "inclusiveness, implementation and investment". China has always positively commented on the various tasks carried out by Turkey during its presidency.

Last November, when I introduced Hangzhou to you in Antalya, I quoted a Chinese saying which goes, "Up in Heaven there is Paradise, down on Earth there are Suzhou and Hangzhou." I believe that the Hangzhou Summit will present you an opportunity to appreciate a unique mixture

---

* Opening speech at the G20 Hangzhou Summit.

of the past and present Hangzhou. Today, this invitation has become a reality. Here we have both old and new friends, as we gather in Hangzhou to discuss major development plans for the world economy.

In the coming two days, we will discuss topics including enhancement of macro-policy coordination, innovation in growth models, more efficient global economic and financial governance, robust international trade and investment, inclusive and interconnected development and other prominent issues that may impact the world economy.

Eight years ago, at the most critical point of the global financial crisis, the world economy was sliding towards a precipice. The G20 was entrusted to pull it back onto a track of stability in a spirit of partnership and joint action. That was an unprecedented move. Unity triumphed over differences. Mutual benefit replaced selfish gains. That crisis made people remember the G20, and led to the establishment of the G20 as the major forum for international economic cooperation.

Eight years later, the world economy has again arrived at a critical moment. Scientific and technological progress, population growth, economic globalization, and other main engines that propelled world economic growth over the past several decades have shifted down a gear, and their impetus for the world economy has visibly weakened. The growth impetus brought about by the previous round of scientific and technological progress has gradually slackened, and a new round of scientific and technological and industrial revolution has yet to gain momentum. A graying society and low population growth rate in major economies have brought about economic and social pressure on various countries. Economic globalization has suffered a setback. Protectionism and inward-looking tendencies have reasserted themselves. The multilateral trading regime has been adversely impacted. In spite of the marked progress in financial oversight reform, risks have continued to accumulate including high leverage and large bubbles. How to make financial markets effectively serve the real economy while maintaining stability still remains a major headache for many countries.

Given the composite effects of these factors, although the world economy has generally maintained a recovery posture, it is still faced with multiple risks and challenges, including a lack of growth impetus, sluggish demand, recurrent volatility in financial markets, and a sustained slump in international trade and investment.

Although the G20 is a forum for the world's major economies with pivotal influences and roles, it also puts itself at the forefront of risks and challenges, and of expanding growth space. The world community has high expectations of the G20 and places great hopes on the current summit. We need to square up to problems and jointly seek answers through respective actions and collective efforts. It is hoped that based on its past achievements, the G20 Hangzhou Summit will offer a prescription that can treat both the symptoms and root causes of the problems and work out comprehensive measures to get the world economy onto a path of robust, sustainable, balanced and inclusive growth.

First, in the face of the current challenges, we should enhance macro-economic policy coordination, join forces to promote global economic growth, and help maintain financial stability. G20 members should adopt sounder and more balanced macro-economic policies in light of their own countries' reality, use various effective policy tools, make overall plans for working out fiscal, monetary and structural reform policies, strive to expand global overall demand, improve the quality of supply in all respects, and solidify the foundation of economic growth. While formulating and implementing the Hangzhou Action Plan, we should continue to enhance policy coordination, reduce negative spillover effects, jointly help maintain financial stability, and raise market confidence.

Second, in the face of the current challenges, we should innovate new development models and tap growth impetus. The G20 should adjust its policy thinking, and place equal emphasis on short-term policies and medium- and long-term policies, as well as on demand-side management and supply-side reform. This year we have reached a consensus on the G20 Blueprint on Innovative Growth, and have unanimously decided to open up a new path and expand new frontiers for the world economy through innovation, structural reforms, new industrial revolution, and digital economy. We need to firmly continue in this direction, help lift the world

economy out of the situation of lackluster recovery and
fragile growth, and lay a solid foundation for a new round of
growth and prosperity.

Third, in the face of the current challenges, we should
improve global economic governance and solidify its mechanism guarantee. The G20 needs to steadily improve the international monetary system, optimize the governance structure
of international financial institutions, and give full play to
the role of SDR of the International Monetary Fund. The
Global Financial Safety Net needs to be improved, and cooperation in financial oversight, international taxation, and
anti-corruption needs to be enhanced so as to increase the
capability of the world economy to resist risks. This year we
have reactivated the G20 international financial framework
working group. We will continue to promote it, and raise its
effectiveness.

Fourth, in the face of the current challenges, we need to
build an open world economy, and continue to push trade
and investment liberalization and facilitation. Protectionism
is like treating an ailment with poison. From a short-term
perspective, protectionism may seem to relieve a country's
internal pressure, but from a long-term perspective, it will
inflict irreparable damage on the country itself and on the
world economy as a whole. The G20 should not adopt
beggar-thy-neighbor policies. Instead, it should advocate and
promote an open world economy, avoid adopting new protectionism measures, strengthen coordination and cooperation
in investment policies, and take effective actions to promote

trade growth. We should give full play to the radiating effect and locomotive roles of infrastructure construction and connectivity, help developing countries and small and medium-sized companies to become part of the global value chain, and push for further opening, exchanges, and integration of the global economy.

Fifth, in the face of the current challenges, we should implement the 2030 Agenda for Sustainable Development, and promote inclusive development. Realizing common development is the hope of the people of all countries, particularly the developing countries. According to available statistics, the world's Gini coefficient is already around 0.7, a figure that is higher than the recognized "danger point" of 0.6. This is something we should pay close attention to. This year we have placed development in a prominent position on the G20 agenda, made a joint commitment to earnest implementation of the 2030 Agenda for Sustainable Development, and formulated action plans. At the same time, we will reduce unequal and imbalanced global development, and enable people of all countries to enjoy the growth results of the world economy by means of supporting the industrialization efforts of Africa and LDCs, enhancing energy access, energy efficiency, the utilization of clean energy and recyclable energy, developing inclusive finance, and encouraging young people to start businesses.

Dear colleagues,

The G20 bears the expectations of various countries. It has important missions. We need to make an effort to build up the G20 and steer the world economy in a sound direction of prosperity and stability.

First, advancing with the times and giving full play to its leading role, the G20 should adjust its own development direction in light of the needs of the world economy and further transform itself from a crisis-management body to a long-term and effective governance mechanism. In the face of major and salient problems, the G20 has the responsibility to play a leadership role, demonstrate a strategic vision, chart a course, and identify a development path for the world economy.

Second, words should be matched with action. We need to adopt pragmatic actions. It is better to enforce one thing than making thousands of commitments. We should make the G20 an action team instead of a talking shop. This year we have formulated action plans in the spheres of sustainable development, green finance, improved energy efficiency, and anti-corruption, and we should implement every action in real earnest.

Third, the G20 should create a platform for cooperation in the spirit of making joint efforts for the benefit of all involved. We should continue to enhance the mechanism building of the G20, to ensure that cooperation will be extended and expanded. It is necessary to extensively seek suggestions, and listen attentively to the voices of countries all around the world, particularly those of the developing countries, so that the G20 will be even more inclusive in its work and it will respond to the appeals of the people of all countries more effectively.

Fourth, the partnership spirit. The partnership spirit is the most precious asset of the G20. Although we may differ in national conditions and development stages, and we may face different challenges, we share the same desire for promoting economic growth, the same intention of addressing crises and challenges, and the same vision for realizing common development. As long as we carry forward the partnership spirit of going through thick and thin together, we will be able to ride through the rough waves of the world economy and embark on a brand-new voyage for future growth.

Dear colleagues,

In the course of preparing for the Hangzhou Summit, China has put into practice the concept of openness, transparency and inclusiveness, and maintained close contact and coordination with all other G20 members. We have also held various forms of parallel dialogue. We have briefed the UN, African Union, Group of 77, LDCs, landlocked countries and small island nations, and given information on our preparations for the Hangzhou Summit to countries all over the world and people who are interested in the G20, and listened attentively to their calls and appeals. Their opinions and suggestions have played an important part in the preparations for this summit.

I expect that in the discussions in the next two days we will pool our wisdom and efforts to make sure that the Hangzhou Summit will realize the objectives of promoting world economic growth, enhancing international economic cooperation, and pushing G20 development.

Let us make the Hangzhou Summit a new starting point, lead the convoy of the world economy on a voyage from the Qiantang River here, and head into the vast ocean.

Thank you all.

Improve Our Ability to Participate in Global Governance*

September 27, 2016

With the increase in global challenges and constant changes in the international balance of power, there is a growing demand for strengthening global governance and transforming the global governance system. We must seize the opportunity and take appropriate actions to foster an international order that is fairer, more equitable, and more rational, and to ensure that the common interests of our country and other developing countries are more securely assured, that external conditions are more favorable for the realization of the Two Centenary Goals and the Chinese Dream of national rejuvenation, and that we make a greater contribution to the noble cause of peace and development of mankind.

Since the 18th CPC National Congress, we have worked proactively to uphold the international order that is based on the purposes and principles of the UN Charter, and safeguard the fruits of victory in World War II that the Chi-

---

* Main points of the speech at the 35th group study session of the Political Bureau of the 18th CPC Central Committee.

nese people won at the expense of great national sacrifice. We have put forward the Belt and Road Initiative, launched new multilateral financial institutions such as the Asian Infrastructure Investment Bank, and facilitated the reform of the IMF quota and governance mechanism. We have also participated actively in creating governance rules in many emerging fields, including the oceans, the polar regions, the internet, outer space, nuclear security, action against corruption, and climate change, and promoted reform of the unfair and unreasonable aspects of the current global governance system.

The recent G20 Hangzhou Summit was the highest-level international summit hosted by China in recent years, unmatched in scale and influence. Leveraging the opportunity to set the agenda, we introduced new initiatives, and guided the summit to produce a series of pioneering, pacesetting and institutional outcomes. We showcased our unique characteristics, and extended our influence. As a result, the summit fulfilled the goal of charting the course for the world economy, providing momentum for global economic growth, and building a solid foundation for international cooperation. The summit provided us with an opportunity for the first time to comprehensively explain our philosophy on global economic governance, taking innovation as the core, giving prominence to development issues in global macroeconomic policy coordination, building a framework of global multilateral investment rules, releasing a president's statement on climate change, and introducing green finance to the G20 agenda. All of this has left a deep imprint of China in the history of the G20.

The pattern of global governance depends on the international balance of power, and the transformation of the global governance system originates from changes in the balance of power. We should take economic development as the central task, pool our efforts to manage our own affairs well, and improve our capability in dealing with international issues. We should actively participate in global governance and shoulder international responsibilities. We must do all we can within the limitations of our capabilities.

The existing global governance system has found it increasingly difficult to meet the requirements of the times, and the international community is calling for reform. This is a common cause of all countries and regions, so we must pursue the transformation of the global governance system by following the principles of extensive consultation, joint contribution, and shared benefits. We must endeavor to reach consensus on the transformation proposals, and turn it into concerted actions. We must continue to voice opinions on behalf of developing countries and strengthen solidarity and cooperation with other developing countries.

We should start from what we are able to do and what is agreed upon. At this stage, we should expand the results of the Hangzhou Summit, reinforce and give full play to the role of the G20 as the main platform for global economic governance, and promote the transformation of the G20 into a long-term governance mechanism. We must continue to promote the Belt and Road Initiative and urge all related parties to strengthen planning and strategic coordination. We should further cooperation within the Shanghai Cooperation Organization, strengthen mechanisms in the Conference on Interaction and Confidence-Building Measures in Asia (CICA), the East Asia Summit, and the ASEAN Regional Forum, and integrate regional free-trade negotiation frameworks. We should also take a more active part in rule-making in emerging fields such as the internet, the polar regions, the deep sea and outer space, and give more support to programs and cooperation mechanisms related to educational exchange, dialogue between civilizations, and ecology.

Since the 18th CPC National Congress, we have advocated the principle of upholding the greater good and pursuing shared interests; and facilitated the building of a new model of international relations featuring cooperation and mutual benefit, a global community of shared future, and a partnership network that links all parts of the world. We have also advocated a common, comprehensive and sustainable security concept based on cooperation. These ideas have been well received in the international community. We should continue to explain to the international community our concept about reform of the global governance system. We will seek cooperation and mutually beneficial results rather than confrontation or zero-sum game. In order to facilitate the transformation of the global governance system, we will try to identify the greatest common denominators, expand cooperation, promote consensus among all parties, and strengthen coordination and cooperation.

We must improve our ability to participate in global governance, and in particular, our ability to make rules, set agendas, and carry out communication and coordination. To play an effective role in global governance we need a large number of professionals who have a good knowledge of the policies and guiding principles of the Party, the government, and the national conditions, have a global outlook, have a good command of foreign languages, have a good understanding of international rules, and are skilled in international negotiations. We should strengthen the training of high-caliber personnel involved in global governance, ensure that we have adequate trained professionals, and build a talent pool, providing personnel support for our participation in global governance.

Make Economic Globalization
More Dynamic, Inclusive and Sustainable[*]

November 19, 2016

Two months ago, a successful G20 Summit was held in Hangzhou, China, during which I and other state leaders had in-depth discussions and reached important consensus on major issues facing the world economy. We expressed concern about the sluggish recovery of the global economy, the lack of growth momentum, the backlash against economic globalization, weak trade and investment, and growing global challenges that cloud the global economic outlook. We agreed that in the face of these risks and challenges, all parties need to work together in a spirit of partnership for win-win outcomes, enhance macro-economic policy coordination, and find creative ways to spur growth, so as to build an open world economy that delivers strong, sustainable, balanced and inclusive growth.

The Asia-Pacific is at a critical stage in which it continues to enjoy steady growth but also faces multiple challenges. With unmatched economic aggregate and vibrancy, the Asia-

---

* Main part of the speech, titled "Enhanced Partnership for Greater Growth Momentum", at the APEC CEO Summit in Lima, Peru.

Pacific must lead the way and take strong and coordinated actions to energize the world economy and create new opportunities for global growth.

First, we should promote an open and integrated economy. Openness is vital to the prosperity of the Asia-Pacific. Thanks to APEC member economies' commitment to trade liberalization and facilitation over the past two decades and more, trade in our region has grown by an average annual rate of 8 percent, more than double the rate of GDP growth in the same period, thus steadily boosting the Asia-Pacific economy.

In recent years, global trade has remained weak. According to WTO forecasts, for the fifth consecutive year global trade may grow slower than GDP in 2016. The Asia-Pacific will come under similar pressure and is grappling with such challenges as the fragmentation of regional economic cooperation. For any regional trade arrangement to gain broad support, it must be open, inclusive, beneficial to all, and achieve win-win results. We need to put in place a framework for regional cooperation featuring equal consultation, joint contribution and shared benefits. Closed and exclusive arrangements are not the right choice.

In this connection, building a Free Trade Area of the Asia-Pacific (FTAAP), which is aptly regarded by the business community as the APEC dream, is a strategic initiative critical to the long-term prosperity of the Asia-Pacific. We should firmly pursue the FTAAP as an institutional mechanism for ensuring an open economy in the Asia-Pacific. We must energize trade and investment to drive growth, make free trade arrangements more open and inclusive, and uphold the multilateral trading regime.

There is now a heated debate about economic globalization, which has both supporters and skeptics. In my view, economic globalization is in keeping with the laws of economics and delivers benefits to all. At the same time, it is a double-edged sword. While driving global development, it has also created new problems and challenges that need to be dealt with. Globally, a new round of scientific, technological and industrial revolution is in the making, change in the international division of labor is accelerating, and global value chains are being reshaped. All these developments have added new dimensions to economic globalization.

APEC was born in the booming years of economic globalization and owes much of its success to this process. We need to recognize the changing dynamics in both our respective countries and the external environment, seize new opportunities, assume new roles, and create new strengths. But globalization gives rise to new issues that deserve serious study. We need to actively guide economic globalization, promote equity and justice, and make economic globalization more dynamic, inclusive and sustainable, so that all will get a fair share of its benefits and all can see that they have a stake in it.

Second, we should enhance connectivity to achieve interconnected development. Connectivity unleashes potential and underpins interconnected development. We need to build a multi-dimensional connectivity network that covers the Asia-Pacific. After eight years, Latin America is again playing host to the APEC meeting. We should seize this opportunity to align the connectivity programs of the two coasts of the Pacific to support and boost the real economy in the whole region. We should follow up on the Connectivity Blueprint adopted at the APEC meeting in Beijing in 2014 and strengthen connectivity in infrastructure, institutions and personnel, so as to make the Asia-Pacific fully connected by 2025.

Three years ago, I proposed the Belt and Road Initiative. It aims to strengthen connectivity to facilitate the free flow of production factors and create a platform of win-win cooperation and shared benefits for all. More than 100 countries and international organizations have joined or expressed support for the initiative, forming a strong "circle of friends" brought together by a common vision, mutual trust, and friendship. The AIIB is up and running. The Silk Road Fund is in place. A number of major projects have been launched, generating huge economic and social benefits. Guided by the principle of extensive consultation, joint contribution and shared benefits, China will work with other parties to promote greater connectivity of policy, transport, trade, currency and people, increase the complementarity of our respective development strategies and expand mutually beneficial cooperation. By doing so, we will drive regional growth and improve people's lives. China welcomes all parties to join this initiative to meet challenges, share opportunities and seek common development.

Third, we should extend reform and innovation to boost our internal driving force. The Asia-Pacific has made great progress in pursuit of development, and every step forward has been made as a result of reform and innovation. Reform and innovation are worthy undertakings, but they are also difficult to accomplish. As an old Chinese saying puts it, the courage to take on challenge will make a difficult job easier. A proverb in Latin America says that there is no greater difficulty than lack of resolve.

In Beijing in 2014, APEC leaders adopted the APEC Accord on Innovative Development, Economic Reform and Growth, charting a course of innovative development for the Asia-Pacific. This year, the G20 Hangzhou Summit adopted the G20 Blueprint on Innovative Growth, highlighting reform and innovation and formulating specific plans of action.

We APEC members should act on this consensus and these principles. We should change the growth model, resolutely adjust the economic structure through reform, and raise total-factor productivity. We should step up macro-policy coordination, firmly advance structural reform, and increase positive spillovers. We should accelerate efforts to explore a new development philosophy, model and pathway, energize social creativity and the market, move our industries and products up the global value chain, and expand the space for development.

Fourth, we should promote win-win cooperation to forge strong partnerships. Partnerships are an important bond for Asia-Pacific cooperation and our natural choice for meeting current challenges. While we all believe that the 21st century is the Asia-Pacific century, good fortune will never befall us of its own accord. Two years ago, APEC leaders reviewed the course of 25 years of APEC cooperation and defined the guiding principles for forging partnerships in the Asia-Pacific. Last year in Manila, we again called for building partnerships in the Asia-Pacific in the spirit of mutual trust, inclusiveness, cooperation and win-win progress.

We should commit ourselves to building a community of shared future. This will bring us closer rather than keeping us apart. We should continue to deepen and expand cooperation in our region. We should build platforms and set rules together and share development outcomes, and any attempt to undercut or exclude each other must be rejected. We should encourage equal participation, full consultation, mutual assistance and common development. Every effort should be made to foster a sound and stable environment for development, and no factor should be allowed to obstruct the development process of the Asia-Pacific.

The common development and prosperity of the Asia-Pacific calls for enhanced cooperation at the regional level and concrete action by each APEC member. China, the world's most populous developing country, has maintained steady and sound growth, thus providing a strong boost to growth in the Asia-Pacific and the rest of the world. Over a period of several years after the outbreak of the international financial crisis in 2008, China contributed almost 40 percent of total global growth, playing a key role in driving global recovery. In recent years, with global growth remaining sluggish, China's economy has encountered some difficulties and challenges. But we have maintained confidence and made proactive adjustments. As a result, China has remained a leader of sustaining growth among major economies and contributed more than 25 percent of overall global growth.

The year 2016 is the first year of China's 13th Five-year Plan. We have adapted to and steered the new normal of economic development, continued to carry out reform across the board, pursued innovation-driven development, and accelerated the shift of our growth model and economic structural adjustment. Thanks to these efforts, China's economy is operating within a sound range. In the first three quarters this year, China's GDP grew by 6.7 percent. Final consumption expenditure contributed to 71 percent of GDP growth. The added value created by services accounted for 52.8 percent of GDP. Energy consumption per unit of GDP dropped by 5.2 percent year on year. A total of 10.67 million urban jobs were created, and the gap between urban and rural incomes continued to narrow. The performance of China's economy has steadily improved; new driving forces are becoming stronger; new forms of businesses are emerging; and many regions and sectors are going through encouraging transformation. All this shows that enabling factors are growing stronger.

China has entered a decisive stage for building a society

of moderate prosperity in all respects. Guided by our vision of innovative, coordinated, green, open and inclusive development, we will prioritize supply-side structural reform, foster a new economic structure, and strengthen new forces driving development to ensure steady and sound economic growth in China.

For the present and the foreseeable future, China will take the following steps in pursuing economic development:

First, we will carry out supply-side structural reform to accelerate the transformation of the growth model. We will drive reform deeper in our economic system, and improve our institutions to ensure that the market will play a decisive role in resource allocation and the government will play a better role. We will increase aggregate demand as called for while advancing structural adjustment through reform. We will promote the reorganization of industries to achieve optimal performance, improve the allocation of production factors, and ensure that the supply structure can better adapt to changes in demand. This will provide steady internal driving forces for sustaining sound growth.

Second, we will promote innovation-driven development and replace old growth drivers with new ones. We will continue to pursue the strategy of innovation-driven development and further scientific and technological system reform to change outdated mindsets and remove institutional obstacles. We will fully leverage the role of science and technology in economic and social development, and tap into all sources of innovation. We will further pool the efforts of businesses,

universities and research institutes to energize business organizations, people, the market and capital to drive innovation-
based development. We will encourage new technologies,
new industries and new businesses so that progress in innovation will be applied in economic activities and converted
into new forces driving growth.

Third, we will promote high-standard, two-way opening up and stick to the principle of mutual benefits. I have
emphasized on many occasions that China will not close its
doors to the outside world, but will open itself even wider.
We will pursue our opening-up strategy with greater resolve
and foster a wide-ranging, deeper and multi-faceted environment of opening up. We will give greater access to foreign
investment and continue to set up high-standard pilot free
trade zones in China. We will further improve the rule-based
and enabling business environment in line with international
standards, and ensure that there is a level playing field for
all companies in China, both domestic and foreign. I am
convinced that these steps will make China's investment
climate more open, more favorable, and more transparent,
thus enabling foreign companies to share in China's growth
opportunities. We encourage more Chinese companies to go
global, increase outbound investment, and set up new platforms for pursuing mutually beneficial cooperation. We will
fully involve ourselves in economic globalization by supporting the multilateral trading regime, advancing the FTAAP,
and working for an early conclusion of the negotiations on
the Regional Comprehensive Economic Partnership.

Fourth, we will promote inclusive and green development to make life better for our people. As an ancient Chinese saying goes, "Bringing benefit to the people is the fundamental principle of governance." There is also a Peruvian saying, "The voice of the people is the voice of God." We should respond to people's aspiration for a better life and ensure that the fruits of development are shared by them. We will improve the mechanism of income redistribution, make the cake bigger and ensure equitable shares, and expand the middle-income group. We will intensify our final fight against poverty so that by 2020, all of the 55.75 million people in rural China remaining under the current poverty line will get rid of poverty. We will redouble efforts to build a healthy China by providing our people with full health services from the cradle to the grave. As we say, clear rivers and green mountains are as valuable as mountains of gold and silver. We will continue to pursue the strategy of sustainable development, promote green, low-carbon and circular development, and build a beautiful China with blue skies, green lands and clear rivers, so that our people can live in a healthy environment created by sound development.

China's economy has excellent prospects, and China's development will present great opportunities to the rest of the world. It is estimated that in the next five years China will import US$8 trillion of goods, introduce US$600 billion of foreign investment and invest US$750 billion overseas, and that Chinese tourists will make over 700 million outbound visits. All of this means a bigger market, more capital, a greater variety of products, and more attractive cooperation opportunities for countries around the world.

Since becoming an APEC member 25 years ago, China has forged ahead alongside other APEC members. Together, we have pursued development and shared prosperity. Together, we have advanced opening up and deepened integration. Together, we have blazed new trails and taken bold initiatives. And together, we have pursued inclusive development based on mutual respect and assistance. Throughout these years, China and the economies in the Asia-Pacific have moved steadily closer to each other. Indeed, China has become a main trading partner and export market for most of the APEC members.

We all know that sweet potato and other varieties of potato originated in Latin America. I once used the sweet potato as an example to make a point to a group of Chinese business leaders. I said that the vines of the sweet potato may stretch in all directions, but they all grow out of its roots. Similarly, no matter what level of development it may reach, China, with its roots in the Asia-Pacific, will continue to contribute to the region's development and prosperity. China is committed to peaceful development and a mutually beneficial strategy of opening up. While striving for its own development, China will also work to promote the common development of all Asia-Pacific countries and create more opportunities for people in our region.

Shoulder the Responsibilities of Our Time and Promote Global Growth Together[*]

January 17, 2017

President Doris Leuthard and Mr Roland Hausin,
Heads of state or government, and deputy heads of state,
Heads of international organizations,
Dr Klaus Schwab and Mrs Hilde Schwab,
Ladies and gentlemen,
Dear friends,

I am delighted to come to beautiful Davos. Davos, though a small town in the Alps, is an important window for taking the pulse of the global economy. People from around the world come here to exchange ideas and insights, which broaden their vision. This makes the World Economic Forum Annual Meeting a cost-effective brainstorming event, which I would call "Schwab economics".

"It was the best of times, it was the worst of times." These are the words used by the English writer Charles Dickens to describe the world after the Industrial Revolution. Today, we also live in a world of contradictions. On

* Keynote speech at the opening ceremony of the World Economic Forum 2017 in Davos, Switzerland.

the one hand, with growing material wealth and advances in science and technology, human civilization has developed as never before. On the other hand, frequent regional conflicts, and global challenges like terrorism, refugees, poverty, unemployment, and a widening income gap have all added to the uncertainties of the world. Many people feel bewildered and ask themselves: What has gone wrong with the world?

To answer this question, one must first track the source of the problem. Some blame economic globalization for the chaos. Economic globalization was once viewed as the treasure cave found by Ali Baba in *The Arabian Nights*, but it has now become a Pandora's box in the eyes of many. The international community finds itself in a heated debate on economic globalization.

Today, I wish to address the global economy in the context of economic globalization.

The point I want to make is that many of the problems troubling the world are not caused by economic globalization. For instance, the refugee waves from the Middle East and North Africa in recent years have become a global concern. Several million people have been displaced, and some small children have lost their lives while crossing the rough sea. This is indeed heartbreaking. It is war, conflict and regional turbulence that have created this problem, and its solution lies in making peace, promoting reconciliation and restoring stability. The global financial crisis is another example. It is not an inevitable outcome of economic globalization; rather, it is the consequence of excessive pursuit of profit by financial capital and a grave failure of financial regulation. Simply blaming economic globalization for the world's problems is neither consistent with reality, nor helpful for finding solutions to the problems.

From the historical perspective, economic globalization is a result of growing social productivity, and a natural outcome of scientific and technological progress – not something created by any individuals or any countries. Economic globalization has powered global growth and facilitated movement of goods and capital, advances in science, technology and civilization, and interactions among peoples.

But we should also recognize that economic globalization is a double-edged sword. When the global economy is under downward pressure, it is hard to make the cake of global economy bigger. It may even shrink, which may cause conflicts between growth and distribution, between capital and labor, and between efficiency and equity. Both developed and developing countries have felt the pinch. Voices against globalization have exposed problems in the process of economic globalization that we need to take seriously.

As a line in an old Chinese poem goes, "Honey melons hang on bitter vines; sweet dates grow on thistles and thorns." In a philosophical sense, nothing is perfect in the world. Those who claim something is perfect because of its merits, or who view something as useless just because of its defects have failed to see the full picture. It is true that economic globalization has created new problems, but this is no justification to write it off altogether. Rather, we should adapt to and guide economic globalization, cushion its negative effects, and make it benefit all countries and all nations.

There was a time when China too had doubts about economic globalization, and was not sure whether it should join the World Trade Organization. But we came to the conclusion that integration with the global economy is a historical trend. To grow its economy, China must have the courage to swim in the vast ocean of the global market. Those who fear to face the storm and explore the new world will sooner or later drown in the ocean. Therefore, China took the bold step to embrace the global market. From time to time we have struggled to keep our heads above the water, and we have encountered whirlpools and choppy waves, but we have learned how to swim in this process. It has proved to be the right strategic choice.

Whether you like it or not, the global economy is the great ocean from which you cannot escape. Any attempt to cut off the flow of capital, technologies, products, industries and people between economies, and channel the waters in the ocean back into isolated lakes and creeks is simply not possible. Indeed, it runs counter to the historical trend.

The history of humanity tells us that problems are not to be feared. What should concern us is refusing to face up to problems and not knowing what to do about them. In the face of both the opportunities and challenges of economic globalization, the right thing to do is to seize every opportunity, jointly meet challenges and chart the right course for economic globalization.

At the APEC Economic Leaders' Meeting in late 2016, I spoke about the need to make the process of economic globalization more vigorous, more inclusive and more sustainable. We should be proactive and manage economic globalization appropriately so as to release its positive impact and keep the process in balance. We should follow the general trend, proceed from our respective national conditions, and embark on the right pathway of integrating with economic globalization at the right pace. We should strike a balance between efficiency and equity to ensure that different countries and different groups of people may all share the benefits of economic globalization. The people of all countries expect nothing less from us, and this is a responsibility we cannot shirk as leaders of our time.

Ladies and gentlemen,

Dear friends,

At present, the most pressing task before us is to steer the global economy out of difficulty. The global economy has remained sluggish for quite some time. The gap between poor and rich and between North and South is widening. The root cause is that the three critical issues in the economic sphere have not been effectively addressed.

First, lack of robust driving forces for growth makes it difficult to sustain a steady growth of the global economy. Global economic growth is now at its slowest pace in seven years. Growth of global trade has been slower than global GDP growth. Short-term policy stimuli are ineffective. Fundamental structural reform is only beginning. The global economy is now in a period of moving towards new growth drivers, and the role of traditional engines to push growth has weakened. Despite the emergence of new technologies such as artificial intelligence and 3D printing, new sources of growth are yet to emerge. A new path for the global economy remains elusive.

Second, inadequate global economic governance makes it difficult to adapt to new developments in the global economy. Mme Christine Lagarde recently told me that emerging markets and developing countries already contribute 80 percent of the growth of the global economy. The global economic landscape has changed profoundly in the past few decades. However, the global governance system has not embraced those new changes and is therefore inadequate in terms of representation and inclusiveness. The global industrial landscape is changing and new industrial chains, value chains and supply chains are taking shape. However, trade and investment rules have not kept pace with these developments, resulting in acute problems such as closed mechanisms and fragmentation of rules. The global financial market needs to be more resilient against risks, but the global financial governance mechanism fails to meet the new requirements and is thus unable to effectively resolve problems such as excess international financial market volatility and the build-up of asset bubbles.

Third, uneven global development makes it difficult to meet people's expectations for better lives. Dr Schwab has observed in his book, *The Fourth Industrial Revolution*, that this round of industrial revolution will produce extensive and far-reaching impacts such as growing inequality, particularly the possible widening gap between return on capital and return on labor. The richest one percent of the world's population owns more wealth than the remaining 99 percent. Inequality in income distribution and uneven development space are worrying. Over 700 million people in the world are still living in extreme poverty. For many families, to have a warm house, adequate food and secure employment is still a distant dream. This is the biggest challenge facing the world today. It is also what is behind the social turmoil in some countries.

All this shows that there are indeed problems with world economic growth, governance and development models, and they must be resolved. Henry Dunant, the founder of the Red Cross, once said, "Our real enemy is not the neighboring country; it is hunger, poverty, ignorance, superstition and prejudice." We need to have the wisdom to dissect these problems; more importantly, we need to have the courage to take actions to address them.

First, we should develop a dynamic, innovation-driven growth model. The fundamental issue plaguing the global economy is the lack of driving force for growth. Innovation is the primary force leading development. Unlike the previous industrial revolutions, the fourth Industrial Revolution is unfolding at an exponential rather than linear rate. We need to chart a new course through innovation. Only with the courage to innovate and reform can we remove bottlenecks blocking global growth and development.

With this in mind, the G20 leaders reached an important consensus at the Hangzhou Summit, which is to take innovation as a key driver and foster a new driving force for growth for both individual countries and the global economy. We should develop new development concepts and go beyond the debate about whether there should be more fiscal stimulus or more monetary easing. We should adopt a multi-pronged, holistic approach to address both the symptoms and the underlying problems. We should adopt new policy instruments and advance structural reform to create more space for growth and sustain its momentum. We should develop new growth models and seize opportunities presented by the new round of industrial revolution and the digital economy. We should meet the challenges of climate change and aging population. We should also address the negative impact of IT and automation on jobs. When cultivating new industries, new business forms, and new business models, we should create new jobs and restore confidence and hope to our peoples.

Second, we should pursue a well-coordinated and interconnected approach to develop a model of open and win-win cooperation. Today, mankind has become a close-knit community of shared future. Countries have extensive converging interests and are mutually dependent. All countries have the right to development. At the same time, they should view their own interests in a broader context and refrain from pursuing their interests at the expense of others.

We should commit ourselves to growing an open global economy, share opportunities and interests through opening up, and achieve win-win outcomes. We should not just retreat to the harbor when encountering a storm, for this will never get us to the other shore of the ocean. We must redouble our efforts to develop global connectivity to enable all countries to achieve inter-connected growth and share prosperity. We must remain committed to developing global free trade and investment, promote trade and investment liberalization and facilitation through opening up, and say no to protectionism. Pursuing protectionism is like locking oneself in a dark room. While wind and rain may be kept outside, the dark room will also block light and air. No one will emerge as a winner in a trade war.

Third, we should develop a model of fair and equitable governance in keeping with the trend of the times. As the Chinese saying goes, shrewd people of petty mind attend to trivial matters, while people with vision attend to the governance of institutions. There is a growing call from the international community for reforming the global economic governance system, which is a pressing task for us. Only when it adapts to new dynamics in the international economic architecture can the global governance system sustain global growth.

Countries, big or small, strong or weak, rich or poor, are all equal members of the international community. As such, they are entitled to participate in decision-making, enjoy rights, and fulfill obligations on an equal basis. Emerging markets and developing countries deserve greater representation and voice. The 2010 IMF quota reform has entered into force, and its momentum should be sustained. We should adhere to multilateralism and uphold the authority and efficacy of multilateral institutions. We should honor commitments and comply with rules. No one should select or bend rules as they see fit. The Paris Agreement is a hard-won achievement which is in keeping with the underlying trend of global development. All signatories should stick to it as this is a responsibility we must assume for future generations.

Fourth, we should develop a balanced, equitable and inclusive development model. As the Chinese saying goes, "When the Great Way rules, the land under Heaven belongs to the people." Development is ultimately for the people. To achieve more balanced development and ensure that the people have equal access to opportunities and to the benefits of development, it is crucial to have a sound development philosophy and model, and make development equitable, effective and balanced.

We should foster a culture that values diligence, frugality and enterprise, and respects the fruits of the hard work of all. Priority should be given to addressing poverty, unemployment, the widening income gap and the concerns of the disadvantaged to promote social equity and justice. It is important to protect the environment while pursuing economic and social progress so as to achieve harmony between humanity and nature and between humanity and society. The

2030 Agenda for Sustainable Development should be implemented to realize balanced development across the world.

A Chinese adage reads, "Victory is ensured when people pool their strength; success is secured when people put their heads together." As long as we keep to the goal of building a global community of shared future and work hand in hand to fulfill our responsibilities and overcome difficulties, we will be able to create a better world and deliver better lives for our peoples.

Ladies and gentlemen,

Dear friends,

China has become the world's second largest economy thanks to 38 years of reform and opening up. The right path leads to a bright future. China has come this far because under the leadership of the CPC, the Chinese people have blazed a development trail that suits China's actual conditions.

This is a path based on China's realities. China has in the past years succeeded in following the appropriate development path by drawing on both the wisdom of its civilization and the practices of other countries in both the East and West. In exploring this path, China has refused to remain insensitive to the changing times or to blindly follow in others' footsteps. All roads lead to Rome. No country should view its own development path as the only viable one, still less should it impose its own development path on others.

This is a path that puts people's interests first. China follows a people-oriented development philosophy and is committed to bettering the lives of its people. Development is of the people, by the people and for the people. China pursues the goal of common prosperity. We have taken major steps to alleviate poverty and lifted over 700 million people out of poverty, and good progress is being made in our efforts to build a society of moderate prosperity in all respects.

This is a path of reform and innovation. China has tackled difficulties and met challenges on its way forward through reform. China has demonstrated the courage to take on difficult issues, navigate treacherous rapids, and remove institutional and systemic hurdles standing in the way of development. These efforts have enabled us to unleash productivity and social vitality. Building on progress of these 30 years and more of reform, we have introduced more than 1,200 reform measures over the past four years, injecting powerful impetus into China's development.

This is a path of pursuing common development through opening up. China is committed to a fundamental policy of opening up and pursues a win-win opening-up strategy. China has promoted an interconnected development, both inward and outward; while developing itself, China has shared its fruit with other countries and peoples.

China's outstanding achievements and the vastly improved living standards of the Chinese people are a blessing to both China and the rest of the world. The achievements through development over the past decades are owed to the hard work and perseverance of the Chinese people, a quality that has defined the Chinese nation for several thousand years. We Chinese know only too well that no one in the world will give us a free ride. For a big country with over 1.3 billion people, development can be achieved only with the dedication and tireless efforts of its own people. We cannot expect others to deliver development to China, and no one is in a position to do so.

When assessing China's development, one should not only see what benefits the Chinese people have gained, but also how much hard effort they have put in; not just what China has achieved, but also what China has contributed to the world. Then one will reach a balanced conclusion about China's development.

Between 1950 and 2016, despite its modest level of development and living standards, China provided more than RMB400 billion of foreign assistance, undertook over 5,000 foreign assistance projects, including nearly 3,000 turn-key projects, and held over 11,000 training workshops in China for over 260,000 personnel from other developing countries. Since it launched reform and opening up, China has attracted over US$1.7 trillion of foreign investment and has made overseas investment totaling over US$1.2 trillion, making a huge contribution to global economic development. In the years following the outbreak of the global financial crisis, China contributed on average to over 30 percent of global growth every year. All these figures are among the highest in the world.

The figures speak for themselves. China's development is an opportunity for the world; China has not only benefited from economic globalization but also contributed to it. Rapid growth in China has been a sustained, powerful engine for global economic stability and expansion. The interconnected development of China and a large number of other countries has made the world economy more balanced. China's remarkable achievement in poverty reduction has contributed to more inclusive global growth. And China's continuous progress in reform and opening up has lent much momentum to an open world economy.

We Chinese know only too well what it takes to achieve prosperity, so we applaud the achievements of others and wish them a better future. We are not jealous of others' success; and we will not complain about others who have benefited so much from the great opportunities presented by China's development. We will open our arms to the people of other countries and welcome them aboard the express train of China's development.

Ladies and gentlemen,

Dear friends,

I know you are all closely following China's economic development, and let me give you an update on the state of China's economy. Our economy has entered what we call a new normal, in which major changes are taking place in terms of growth rate, development model, economic structure and drivers of growth.

But the economic fundamentals sustaining sound development remain unchanged. Despite a sluggish global economy, China's economy is expected to grow by 6.7 percent in 2016, still one of the highest rates in the world. China's economy is far bigger in size than in the past, and the driving force behind it today could not be reached at the time when we had double-digit growth. Household consumption and the service sector have become the main drivers of growth. In the first three quarters of 2016, the added value of the tertiary industry made up 52.8 percent of GDP and domestic consumption contributed 71 percent of economic growth. Household incomes and employment have steadily risen, while per unit GDP energy consumption has continued to drop. Our efforts to pursue green development are paying off.

The Chinese economy faces certain downward pressure and many difficulties, including an acute mismatch between excess capacity and an upgrading demand structure, lack of internal drivers for growth, an accumulation of financial risks, and growing challenges in certain regions. We see these as temporary hardships that occur on the way forward. And the measures we have taken to address these problems are producing good results. We are firm in our resolve to forge ahead. China is the world's largest developing country with over 1.3 billion people, and their living standards are not yet high. But this reality also means China has enormous potential and space for development. Guided by the vision of innovative, coordinated, green, open and inclusive development, we will adapt to the new normal, stay ahead of the curve, and make coordinated efforts to maintain steady growth, accelerate reform, adjust economic structure, improve people's living standards and fend off risks. With these efforts, we aim to maintain a medium-to-high rate of growth and upgrade the economy to the higher end of the value chain.

– China will strive to enhance the performance of economic growth. We will pursue supply-side structural reform as the general goal, shift the growth model, and upgrade the economic structure. We will continue to cut overcapacity, reduce inventory, deleverage financing, reduce costs, and strengthen weak links. We will foster new drivers of growth, develop an advanced manufacturing sector and upgrade the real economy. We will implement the Internet Plus action plan to boost effective demand and better meet the individualized and diverse needs of consumers. And we will do more to protect the ecosystem.

– China will boost market vitality to add new impetus to growth. We will intensify reform in priority areas and key links and enable the market to play a decisive role in resource allocation. Innovation will continue to feature prominently on our growth agenda. In pursuing the strategy of innovation-driven development, we will bolster the strategic emerging industries, apply new technologies and foster new business models to upgrade traditional industries; and we will boost new drivers of growth and revitalize traditional ones.

– China will foster an enabling and orderly environment for investment. We will ease market access for foreign investors, build high-standard pilot free trade zones, strengthen protection of property rights, and level the playing field to make China's market more transparent and better regulated.

In the coming five years, China is expected to import US$8 trillion of goods, attract US$600 billion of foreign direct investment and make US$750 billion of outbound investment. Chinese tourists will make 700 million overseas visits. All this will create a bigger market, more capital, more products and more business opportunities for other countries. China's development will continue to offer opportunities to business communities in other countries. China will keep its doors wide open. An open door allows both other countries to access the Chinese market and China itself to integrate with the world. And we hope that other countries will also keep their doors open to Chinese investors and keep the playing field level for us.

– China will vigorously foster an environment of opening up for common development. We will advance the building of the Free Trade Area of the Asia-Pacific and negotiations on the Regional Comprehensive Economic Partnership to form a network of free trade arrangements that is oriented towards the wider world. China stands for concluding open, transparent and mutually beneficial regional free trade arrangements and opposes forming exclusive groups that are fragmented in nature. China has no intention of boosting its trade competitiveness by devaluing the Renminbi, still less will it launch a currency war.

More than three years ago, I proposed the Belt and Road Initiative. Since then, over 100 countries and international organizations have responded to it positively and supported the initiative. More than 40 countries and international organizations have signed cooperation agreements with China, and our circle of friends along the Belt and Road is growing larger. Chinese companies have made over US$50 billion of investment and launched a number of major projects in the countries along the routes, spurring the economic development of these countries, and creating many jobs locally. The Belt and Road Initiative originated in China, but it has benefitted countries well beyond its borders.

In May this year, China will host in Beijing the Belt and Road Forum for International Cooperation, which aims to discuss ways to boost cooperation, build cooperation platforms and share cooperation outcomes. The forum will also explore ways to address problems facing the global and regional economies, create fresh energy for pursuing interconnected development, and ensure that the Belt and Road Initiative delivers greater benefits to people of countries involved.

Ladies and gentlemen,

Dear friends,

World history shows that the road of human civilization has never been a smooth one, and that humanity has made progress by surmounting difficulties. No difficulty, however daunting, will stop us from advancing. When encountering difficulties, we should not complain about ourselves, blame others, lose confidence or shirk our responsibilities. We should join hands and rise to the challenge. History is created by the brave. Let us boost confidence, take action and march arm-in-arm towards a bright future.

Thank you all.

Towards a Global Community of Shared Future[*]

January 18, 2017

Your Excellency Mr Peter Thomson, President of the 71st
    Session of the UN General Assembly,
Your Excellency Mr António Guterres, UN Secretary General,
Your Excellency Mr Michael Møller, Director General of the
    UN Office at Geneva,
Ladies and gentlemen,
Dear friends,

As a new year begins, everything takes on a new look, and it gives me great pleasure to visit the United Nations Office at Geneva and discuss with you a global community of shared future, which is the call of our time.

I have just attended the World Economic Forum Annual Meeting. In Davos, many speakers pointed out that today's world is full of uncertainties. They observed that people long for a bright future but are bewildered about what lies ahead. What has happened to the world and how should we respond? The world is reflecting on these questions, and they are also very much on my mind.

---

[*] Speech at the United Nations Office at Geneva.

I believe that to answer these questions, we need to be clear about fundamental issues: Where did we come from? Where are we now? And where are we going?

Over the past century and more, humanity has gone through blood-drenched hot wars and the chilling Cold War, but has also achieved remarkable development and huge progress. In the first half of last century, humanity suffered the scourges of two world wars, and the people yearned for the end of war and the advent of peace. In the 1950s and 1960s, the peoples of the colonies awakened and fought to shake off their shackles and achieve independence. Since the end of the Cold War, people have pursued a shared aspiration to expand cooperation for common development.

Peace and development have been the aspirations held dear by all humanity over the past century or more. However, the goal is far from being met. We need to respond to the people's call, take up the baton of history, and forge ahead on the marathon track towards peace and development.

Humanity is in an era of major development, transformation, and adjustment. The trend towards multipolarity and economic globalization is surging. Progress is being made in the application of IT in social development and in the promotion of cultural diversity. A new round of scientific and industrial revolution is in progress. Interconnection and interdependence between countries are crucial for human survival. The forces of peace far outweigh factors causing war, and the trend of our times towards peace, development, cooperation, and win-win outcomes has gained stronger momentum.

On the other hand, humanity is also in an era of numerous challenges and increasing risks. Global growth is sluggish, the impact of the financial crisis lingers on, and the development gap is widening. Armed conflicts occur from time to time. Cold War mentality and power politics still exist. Nonconventional security threats, particularly terrorism, refugee crises, major communicable diseases and climate change, are spreading.

There is only one Earth and we humans have only one home. Dr Stephen Hawking has raised the possibility of parallel universes. He also believes we should seek out other planets that might serve us as new home. We do not know when that hope will come true. For the time being Earth is still the only home we have, so to care for and cherish it is our only option. There is a Latin motto inscribed in the dome of the Federal Palace of Switzerland which says "Unus pro omnibus, omnes pro uno" (One for all, and all for one). We should not only think about our own generation, but also take responsibility for those to come.

Ladies and gentlemen,

Dear friends,

Pass on the torch of peace from generation to generation, sustain development and ensure civilization flourishes: This is what people of all countries long for; it is also the responsibility that statespersons of our generation ought to shoulder. And China stands for building a global community of shared future and achieving inclusive and win-win development.

Vision guides action, and direction determines the future. As modern history shows, to establish a fair and equitable international order is the goal for which humanity has always striven. From the principles of equality and sovereignty established in the Peace of Westphalia over 360 years ago to international humanitarianism affirmed in the Geneva Convention more than 150 years ago; from the four purposes and seven principles enshrined in the UN Charter more than 70 years ago to the Five Principles of Peaceful Coexistence championed by the Bandung Conference over 60 years ago, many principles have emerged in the evolution of international relations and have been widely accepted. These principles should guide us in building a global community of shared future.

Sovereign equality has been the most important norm governing state-to-state relations over the past centuries, and the cardinal principle observed by the United Nations and its agencies and institutions. The essence of sovereign equality is that the sovereignty and dignity of all countries, whether big or small, strong or weak, rich or poor, must be respected; their internal affairs brook no interference, and they have the right to independently choose their social system and development path. In organizations such as the United Nations, World Trade Organization, World Health Organization, World Intellectual Property Organization, World Meteorological Organization, International Telecommunication Union, Universal Postal Union, International Organization for Migration and International Labor Organization, all countries should have an equal voice in decision-making, and they constitute an important force for improving global governance. In a new era, we should uphold sovereign equality and work for the equality of all countries in enjoying rights and opportunities and in making and observing rules.

Geneva witnessed the adoption of the Final Declaration on the Problem of Restoring Peace in Indo-China, the first summit meeting for reconciliation between the two blocs during the Cold War, and the dialogue and negotiations on sensitive issues like the Iranian nuclear issue and the Syrian issue. What we can learn from both past and present is that dialogue and consultation are an effective way to bridge differences, and political negotiation is the fundamental solution to conflicts. When we have sincerity, goodwill, and political wisdom, no conflict is too big to settle and no ice is too thick to break.

An ancient Chinese philosopher said, "Law is the very foundation of governance." Here in Geneva, on the basis of the UN Charter, member states of the United Nations have concluded a number of international conventions and legal instruments on political security, trade, development, social issues, human rights, science and technology, health, labor, intellectual property, culture and sports. The relevance of law lies in its enforcement. It is thus incumbent on all member states to uphold the authority of the international rule of law, exercise their rights in accordance with the law, and fulfill their obligations in good faith. The relevance of law also lies in fairness and justice. All UN member states and international judicial institutions should ensure equal and uniform application of international law and reject double standards or selective application of international law, thus ensuring genuine equality and justice in the world.

As a Chinese saying goes, "The ocean is vast because it admits all rivers." Openness and inclusiveness have made Geneva a center of multilateral diplomacy. We should advance democracy in international relations and reject dominance by just one or a few countries. All countries are entitled to shape the future of the world, making international rules, managing global affairs and sharing the fruits of development.

In 1862, in his book *Un Souvenir de Solférino*, Mr Henry Dunant wondered whether it was possible to set up humanitarian organizations and conclude humanitarian conventions. The answer came one year later with the founding of the International Committee of the Red Cross. Over the past 150 years and more, the Red Cross has become a symbol and a banner. In the face of frequent humanitarian crises, we should champion the spirit of humanity, compassion, and dedication, and give love and hope to innocent people caught in dire situations. We should uphold the basic principles of neutrality, impartiality, and independence, refrain from politicizing humanitarian issues, and ensure non-militarization of humanitarian assistance.

Ladies and gentlemen,

Dear friends,

Great visions can be realized only through actions. Actions

hold the key to building a global community of shared future. To achieve this goal, the international community should promote partnership, security, growth, inter-civilization exchanges and the building of sound ecosystems.

– We should build a world of lasting peace through dialogue and consultation. When countries enjoy peace, so will the world; when countries fight, the world suffers. From the Peloponnesian War in the fifth century BC to the two world wars and the Cold War that lasted more than four decades, we have drawn painful and profound lessons. As a Chinese saying goes, "History, if not forgotten, can serve as a guide for the future." Established by those before us, the United Nations has made it possible for us to enjoy relative peace for more than 70 years. What we need to do is to improve the mechanisms and means to more effectively resolve disputes, reduce tension, and prevent wars and conflicts.

The Swiss writer and Nobel laureate Hermann Hesse stressed the importance of serving "not war and destruction but peace and reconciliation". Countries should foster partnerships based on dialogue, non-confrontation and non-alliance. Major powers should respect each other's core interests, take care of their main concerns, keep their differences under control, and build a new model of relations featuring non-conflict, non-confrontation, mutual respect, and win-win cooperation. As long as we maintain communication and treat each other with sincerity, we can avoid the Thucydides trap. Big countries should treat smaller ones as equals instead of acting as hegemons imposing their will on others. No country should open Pandora's box by willfully launching wars or undermining the international rule of law. Nuclear weapons, the Sword of Damocles that hangs over humanity, should be completely prohibited and thoroughly destroyed over time. Guided by the principles of peace, sovereignty, inclusiveness and shared governance, we should turn the deep sea, the polar regions, outer space and the internet into new frontiers for cooperation rather than a wrestling ground for competition.

– We should build a world of common security for all through joint efforts. No country in the world can enjoy absolute security alone. A country cannot have security while others are in turmoil, as threats facing other countries are likely to haunt it too. When neighbors are in trouble, instead of strengthening one's own fences, one should extend a helping hand to them. As a saying goes, "United we stand, divided we fall." All countries should pursue common, comprehensive, and sustainable security through cooperation.

The terrorist attacks that have occurred in Europe, North Africa and the Middle East in recent years once again demonstrate that terrorism is the common enemy of humanity. Fighting terrorism is the shared responsibility of all countries. In fighting terror, we should not only treat the symptoms, but also remove the root causes. We should enhance coordination and build a global united front against terrorism so as to create an umbrella of security for people around the world.

The number of refugees has hit a record high since the

end of World War II. While tackling the crisis, we should also get to its roots. Why would anyone want to be displaced if they have a home to return to? UNHCR and the International Organization for Migration should act as the coordinator to mobilize the world to respond effectively to the refugee crisis. China has decided to provide an additional RMB200 million in humanitarian assistance for refugees and the displaced of Syria.

As terrorism and refugee crises are closely linked to geopolitical conflicts, resolving conflicts provides the fundamental solution to these problems. Parties that are directly involved in the conflicts should return to the negotiating table, while others should facilitate peace talks. We should all respect the role of the United Nations as the main mediator.

Pandemic diseases such as bird flu, Ebola and Zika have sounded the alarm for international health security. The WHO should play a leadership role in strengthening epidemic monitoring and in sharing information, best practices and technologies. The international community should step up support and assistance for public health in African countries and other developing countries.

　– We should build a world of common prosperity through win-win cooperation. Development is the top priority for all countries. Instead of beggaring their neighbors, countries should stick together like passengers in the same boat. All countries – the main economies in particular – should strengthen macro-policy coordination, pursue both current and long-term interests, and focus on resolving deep-seated problems. We should seize the historic opportunity presented by the new scientific and technological revolution and industrial transformation, shift growth models, drive growth through innovation, and further unleash productivity and creativity. We should uphold WTO rules, support an open, transparent, inclusive, and nondiscriminatory multilateral trading regime, and build an open world economy. Trade protectionism and self-isolation will benefit no one.

Economic globalization, a surging historical trend, has greatly facilitated trade, investment, flow of people, and technological advances. Since the turn of the century, under the auspices of the UN and riding on the waves of economic globalization, the international community has set the Millennium Development Goals and the 2030 Agenda for Sustainable Development. Thanks to these initiatives, 1.1 billion people have been lifted out of poverty, 1.9 billion people now have access to safe drinking water, 3.5 billion people have gained access to the internet, and the goal has been set to eradicate extreme poverty by 2030. All this demonstrates that economic globalization is generally good. Of course, there are still problems, such as development disparity, governance dilemma, digital divide, and equity deficit. But they are growing pains. We should face these problems squarely and tackle them. As we Chinese like to say, "One should not stop eating for fear of choking."

We should draw inspiration from history. Historians told us long ago that rapid economic development necessitates social reform; but people tend to support the former while rejecting the latter. Instead of watching and hesitating, we should move forward against all odds. Answers can also be found in reality. The 2008 global financial crisis has taught us that we should strengthen coordination and improve governance so as to ensure sound growth of economic globalization and make it open, inclusive, balanced and beneficial to all. We should make the cake bigger and share it fairly to ensure justice and equity.

Last September, the G20 Summit in Hangzhou focused on global economic governance and other major issues, adopted the Blueprint on Innovative Growth, put development for the first time in the global macro-policy framework, and formulated an action plan.

– We should build an open and inclusive world through exchanges and mutual learning. "Delicious soup is made by combining different ingredients." Diversity in human civilizations not only defines our world, but also drives human progress. There are more than 200 countries and regions, over 2,500 ethnic groups, and multiple religions in our world. Different histories, national conditions, ethnic groups and customs give birth to different civilizations and make the world colorful. There is no such thing as a superior or inferior civilization. Civilizations are different only in identity and location. Diversity in civilizations should not be a source of global conflict; rather, it should be a driver for progress.

Every civilization, with its own appeal and roots, is a human treasure. Diverse civilizations should draw on each other to achieve common progress. Exchanges among civilizations should become a source of inspiration for advancing human society and a bond that keeps the world in peace.

– We should make our world clean and beautiful by pursuing green and low-carbon development. Humanity coexists with nature, which means that any harm to nature will eventually come back to haunt humanity. We hardly notice natural resources such as air, water, soil and blue sky when we have them. But we will not survive without them. Industrialization has created material wealth as never seen before, but it has also inflicted irreparable damage on the environment. We must not exhaust all the resources passed on to us by previous generations and leave nothing to our children, or pursue development in a destructive way. Clear waters and green mountains are as good as mountains of gold and silver. We must maintain harmony between man and nature and pursue sustainable development.

We should pursue a green, low-carbon, circular, and sustainable way of life and work, advance the 2030 Agenda for Sustainable Development in a balanced manner, and explore a model of sound development that ensures growth, better lives and a good environment. The Paris Agreement is a milestone in the history of climate governance. We must ensure this endeavor is not derailed. All parties should work together to implement the Paris Agreement. China will continue to take steps to tackle climate change and fully honor its obligations.

The Swiss Army Knife embodies Swiss craftsmanship. When I first got one, I was amazed that it had so many devices.

I could not help thinking how wonderful it would be if an exquisite Swiss Army Knife could be made for our world. Whenever there is a problem, we could use one of the tools on the knife to fix it. I believe that with a ceaseless effort on the part of the international community, such a knife can be created.

Ladies and gentlemen,

Dear friends,

We in China always believe that China will do well only when the world does well, and vice versa. Many people are interested in what policies China will pursue, and are speculating on the subject. Here, I wish to give you an explicit answer.

First, China remains unchanged in its commitment to world peace. Amity with neighbors, harmony without uniformity, and peace are values very much cherished in Chinese culture. *The Art of War*, a Chinese classic, begins with this observation, "The art of war is of vital importance to the state. It is a matter of life and death, a road to either survival or ruin. Hence it demands careful study." What this means is that every effort should be made to prevent a war and great caution must be exercised when it comes to fighting a war. For several millennia, peace has been in the blood of us Chinese and a part of our DNA.

Even when China was so strong that its GDP accounted for 30 percent of the global total several centuries ago, it was never engaged in aggression or expansion. In the century following the Opium War of 1840, China suffered immensely from aggression, wars and chaos. Confucius said, "Do not do unto others what you do not want others to do unto you." We Chinese firmly believe that peace and stability are the only way to development and prosperity.

China has grown from a poor and weak country to the second largest economy not through military expansion or colonial plunder, but through the hard work of its people and their efforts to uphold peace. China will never waver in its pursuit of peaceful development. No matter how strong its economy grows, China will never seek hegemony, expansion or spheres of influence. History has borne this out and will continue to do so.

Second, China remains unchanged in its commitment to pursuing common development. As an old Chinese saying goes, "When you reap fruits, you should remember the tree; when you drink water, you should remember its source." China has benefited from the world in its development, and China has also contributed to the world's development.

We will continue to pursue a mutually beneficial opening-up strategy, share our development opportunities with other countries and welcome them on board the train of China's development.

Between 1950 and 2016, China provided foreign countries with over RMB400 billion in aid, and we will continue to increase assistance to them as far as our ability permits. Since the outbreak of the global financial crisis, China has contributed on average over 30 percent of global growth each year. In the coming five years, China is expected to import

US$8 trillion worth of goods, attract US$600 billion in foreign investment, and make US$750 billion in outbound investment. It is also expected that Chinese tourists will make 700 million outbound visits. All this means more development opportunities for other countries.

China pursues development in light of its national conditions. We always put people's rights and interests above everything else and have worked hard to promote and protect human rights. China has met the basic living needs of its 1.3 billion-plus people and lifted over 700 million people out of poverty, which is a significant contribution to the global cause of human rights.

The Belt and Road Initiative that I have proposed aims to achieve win-win and shared development. Over 100 countries and international organizations have positively responded to and supported the initiative, and a large number of "early harvest" projects have been launched. China supports the successful operation of the Asian Infrastructure Investment Bank and other new multilateral financial institutions in order to provide more public goods to the international community.

Third, China remains unchanged in its commitment to fostering partnerships. China pursues an independent foreign policy of peace, and is ready to enhance friendship and cooperation with all other countries on the basis of the Five Principles of Peaceful Coexistence. China is the first country to make partnership-building a principle guiding its relations with other countries. It has formed partnerships of various forms with over 90 countries and regional organizations, and will expand its circle of friends around the world.

China will promote efforts to put in place a framework of major-country relations featuring general stability and balanced growth. We will strive to build a new model of major-country relations with the United States, a comprehensive strategic partnership of coordination with Russia, a partnership for peace, growth, reform and civilization with Europe, and a partnership of unity and cooperation with other BRICS countries. China will continue to uphold the greater good and pursue shared interests, and boost pragmatic cooperation with other developing countries to achieve common development. We will further enhance mutually beneficial cooperation with our neighbors based on amity, sincerity, mutual benefit, and inclusiveness. We will pursue common development with African countries in a spirit of sincerity, affinity and good faith and with a result-oriented approach. And we will elevate our comprehensive cooperative partnership with Latin America to a higher level.

Fourth, China remains unchanged in its commitment to multilateralism. Multilateralism is an effective way to peace and development. For decades, the United Nations and other international institutions have made a universally recognized contribution to maintaining global peace and sustaining development.

China is a founding member of the United Nations, and it was the first country to put its signature on the UN Charter. China will firmly uphold the international system with the UN at its core, the fundamental norms governing international relations embodied in the purposes and principles of the UN Charter, the authority and stature of the UN, and its core role in international affairs.

The China-UN Peace and Development Fund has been formally inaugurated. We will make funds available to peace and development oriented programs proposed by the UN and its agencies in Geneva on a priority basis. China will increase its support for multilateralism as the country continues to develop itself.

Ladies and gentlemen,

Dear friends,

Geneva invokes a special memory in us. In 1954, Premier Zhou Enlai led a delegation to the Geneva Conference, and worked with the Soviet Union, the United States, the United Kingdom and France for a political settlement to the Korean issue and a ceasefire in Indo-China. This demonstrated China's desire for peace and contributed Chinese wisdom to world peace. Since 1971, when China regained its lawful seat in the UN and began to return to Geneva-based international agencies, we have gradually involved ourselves in disarmament, trade, development, human rights and social issues, offering Chinese proposals for the resolution of major issues and the making of important rules. In recent years, China has taken an active part in dialogues and negotiations on the Iranian nuclear issue, the Syrian issue, and other flashpoints, giving Chinese input to their political settlement. China applied to the International Olympic Committee to host both the summer and winter Olympic games and the Paralympics, and we won the bids. In addition, we have gained endorsement from the International Union for Conservation of Nature for over a dozen applications for world natural heritage sites as well as world cultural and natural heritage sites. All this has presented Chinese splendor to the world.

Ladies and gentlemen,

Dear friends,

As an ancient Chinese saying goes, "One should be good at finding the laws of things and solving problems." Building a community of shared future is an exciting goal, and it requires efforts from generation to generation. China is ready to work with all the other UN member states as well as international organizations and agencies to advance the great cause of building a global community of shared future.

On January 28, we Chinese will celebrate the Chinese New Year, the Year of the Rooster. The rooster symbolizes bright prospects and auspiciousness. As a Chinese saying goes, "The crow of the golden rooster heralds a great day for all." With that, I wish you all the very best and a very happy Chinese New Year.

Thank you.

Work Together to Build the Belt and Road[*]

May 14, 2017

Distinguished heads of state or government,

Heads of international organizations,

Ladies and gentlemen,

Dear friends,

In this lovely season of early summer when every living thing is full of energy, I wish to welcome all of you, distinguished guests representing over 100 countries, to this forum on the Belt and Road Initiative in Beijing. This is indeed a gathering of great minds. In the coming two days, I hope that we will fully exchange views and contribute our ideas on how to pursue the Belt and Road Initiative, a project of the century, which will benefit people across the world.

Ladies and gentlemen,

Dear friends,

Over 2,000 years ago, our ancestors, trekking across vast steppes and deserts, opened the transcontinental passage connecting Asia, Europe and Africa, known today as the Silk Road. Our ancestors, navigating rough seas, created sea

---

* Speech at the opening ceremony of the Belt and Road Forum for International Cooperation in Beijing.

routes linking the East with the West, namely, the Maritime Silk Road. The ancient Silk Road, embracing both the land silk road and maritime silk route, opened windows of friendly engagement between nations, adding a splendid chapter to the history of human progress. The thousand-year-old gilt bronze silkworm displayed at China's Shaanxi History Museum and the Belitung shipwreck discovered in Indonesia bear witness to this exciting period of history.

Spanning thousands of miles and years, the ancient Silk Road embodies the spirit of peace and cooperation, openness and inclusiveness, mutual learning and mutual benefit. The Silk Road spirit has become a great heritage of human civilization.

– Peace and cooperation. In China's Han Dynasty, around 130 BC, Zhang Qian, an imperial emissary, left Chang'an, capital of the Han Dynasty. He traveled westward on a mission of peace, and opened an overland route linking the East and the West, a daring undertaking which came to be known as Zhang Qian's journey to the Western Regions. Centuries later, during the Tang, Song and Yuan dynasties, the Silk Road, by both land and sea, became increasingly busy. Great adventurers, including Du Huan of China, Marco Polo of Italy and Ibn Battuta of Morocco, left their footprints along these ancient routes. In the early 15th century, Zheng He, the famous Chinese navigator of the Ming Dynasty, made seven voyages to the Western Seas, a feat which is still remembered today. These pioneers won their place in history not as conquerors with warships, guns or swords.

Rather, they are remembered as friendly emissaries leading camel caravans and sailing treasure-laden ships. Generation after generation, the Silk Road travelers built a bridge for peace and East-West cooperation.

– Openness and inclusiveness. The ancient Silk Road spanned the valleys of the Nile, the Tigris and Euphrates, the Indus and Ganges, and the Yellow and Yangtze rivers. They connected the birthplaces of the Egyptian, Babylonian, Indian and Chinese civilizations, the lands of Buddhism, Christianity and Islam, and homes of people of different ethnic groups and races. Through the Silk Road, people of different civilizations, religions and races interacted with and embraced each other with open minds, in the spirit of seeking common ground while reserving differences. In the course of exchanges, they fostered a spirit of mutual respect and were engaged in a common endeavor to pursue prosperity. Today, the ancient cities of Jiuquan, Dunhuang, Turfan, Kashi, Samarkand, Baghdad and Constantinople, as well as the ancient ports of Ningbo, Quanzhou, Guangzhou, Beihai, Colombo, Jeddah and Alexandria stand as living monuments to these past interactions. This part of history shows that civilization thrives with openness and nations prosper through exchanges.

– Mutual learning. The ancient Silk Road was not for trade only; it boosted the flow of knowledge as well. Through the Silk Road, Chinese silk, porcelain, lacquerware and ironware were shipped to the West, while pepper, flax, spices, grapes and pomegranates entered China. Through the

Silk Road, Buddhism, Islam and Arab astronomy, calendar and medicine found their way to China, while China's Four Great Inventions (paper-making, gunpowder, printing and the compass) and silkworm breeding spread to other parts of the world. More importantly, the exchange of goods and know-how spurred new ideas. For example, Buddhism originated in India, blossomed in China and was enriched in Southeast Asia. Confucianism, which originated in China, gained appreciation by European thinkers such as Leibniz and Voltaire. Herein lie the appeal of mutual learning and the fruit of exchanges.

– Mutual benefit. The ancient Silk Road witnessed bustling scenes of visiting emissaries and traveling merchants jostling one another on the land and numerous ships calling at ports. Along these major arteries of interaction, capital, technology and people flowed freely, and goods, resources and culture were shared widely. The important ancient cities of Alma-Ata, Samarkand and Chang'an prospered, and the Port of Sur and Guangzhou Port thrived, as did the Roman Empire and the Parthian and Kushan kingdoms. The Han and Tang dynasties of China were a golden age. The ancient Silk Road brought prosperity and development to these regions.

History is our best teacher. The glory of the ancient Silk Road shows that geographical distance is not insurmountable. If we take the first courageous step towards each other, we can embark on a path leading to friendship, shared development, peace, harmony and a better future.

Ladies and gentlemen,

Dear friends,

From the historical perspective, mankind has reached an age of major development, transformation, and adjustment. In this increasingly multipolar, economically globalized, digitized and culturally diversified world, the trend towards peace and development has become stronger, and reform and innovation are gaining momentum. Never have we seen such close interdependence between countries as today, and such a fervent desire of people for a better life, and never have we had so many means to prevail over difficulties.

In terms of reality, we find ourselves in a world fraught with challenges. Global economic growth requires new drivers, development needs to be more inclusive and balanced, and the gap between rich and poor needs to be narrowed. Flashpoints in some regions are causing instability, and terrorism is rampant. Deficits in the spheres of peace, development and governance have posed daunting challenges to humanity. All this has always been on my mind.

In the fall of 2013, I proposed building the Silk Road Economic Belt in Kazakhstan and the 21st Century Maritime Silk Road in Indonesia, which is now known as the Belt and Road Initiative. As a Chinese saying goes, "Peaches and plums do not speak, but they are so attractive that a path is formed below the trees." Four years on, over 100 countries and international organizations have become involved in this initiative. Important resolutions passed by the UN General Assembly and Security Council contain references to it. Thanks to our efforts, the Belt and Road Initiative is becoming a reality and bearing rich fruit.

– These four years have seen deeper policy coordination. I have said on many occasions that the Belt and Road Initiative is not meant to reinvent the wheel. Rather, it aims to leverage the comparative strengths of the countries involved and coordinate their development strategies. We have enhanced policy coordination with relevant countries for such initiatives as the Eurasian Economic Union proposed by Russia, the Master Plan on Connectivity by ASEAN, the Bright Road initiative by Kazakhstan, the Middle Corridor initiative by Turkey, the Development Road initiative by Mongolia, the Two Corridors, One Economic Circle initiative by Viet Nam, the Northern Powerhouse initiative by the UK, and the Amber Road initiative by Poland. We are also promoting the coordination of the national development plans of China, Laos, Cambodia, Myanmar, Hungary and many other countries. China has signed cooperation agreements with over 40 countries and international organizations, and institutionalized cooperation in industrial capacity with more than 30 countries. During the forum, a number of agreements on policy coordination and action plans will be signed. We will also launch the Belt and Road cooperation initiative on trade cooperation together with some 60 countries and international organizations. Such policy coordination will have a multiplying effect on cooperation among the parties involved.

– These four years have seen enhanced infrastructure connectivity. Building roads and railways helps create prosperity in all sectors. We have accelerated the implementation of such projects as the Jakarta-Bandung high-speed railway, China-Laos railway, Addis Ababa-Djibouti railway, Hungary-Serbia railway, and Gwadar and Piraeus ports in cooperation with the relevant countries. In addition, a large number of connectivity projects are in the pipeline. Today, a multi-dimensional infrastructure network is taking shape, one that is underpinned by economic corridors such as the China-Pakistan Economic Corridor, China-Mongolia-Russia Economic Corridor and New Eurasian Continental Bridge, connected by land-sea-air transportation routes and information expressways, and supported by major railway, port and pipeline projects.

– These four years have seen increased trade cooperation. China has worked with other countries involved in the Belt and Road Initiative to promote trade and investment and improve the business environment. I was told that for Kazakhstan and other Central Asian countries alone, customs clearance time for agricultural produce being exported to China has been cut by 90 percent. Total trade between China and other Belt and Road countries in 2014-2016 exceeded US$3 trillion-worth, and China's investment in Belt and Road countries has surpassed US$50 billion. Chinese companies have set up 56 economic and trade cooperation zones in over 20 countries, generating some US$1.1 billion in tax revenue and 180,000 jobs.

– These four years have seen expanded financial integration. Financing bottlenecks are a key challenge to realizing connectivity. China has engaged in multiple forms of financial cooperation with countries and organizations involved in the Belt and Road Initiative. The AIIB has provided US$1.7 billion in loans for nine projects in participating countries. The Silk Road Fund has invested US$4 billion in those countries, and the Sino-CEEC Financial Holding Company Limited, or a "16+1" arrangement, has been officially inaugurated. With a distinctive focus, these new financial mechanisms and traditional multilateral financial institutions such as the World Bank complement each other. A basic multi-tiered Belt and Road financial integration network has taken shape.

– These four years have seen increased people-to-people contacts. Friendship, which derives from close contacts between peoples, holds the key to sound state-to-state relations. Guided by the Silk Road spirit, we, countries participating in the Belt and Road Initiative, have pooled our efforts to build the educational Silk Road and the health Silk Road, and carried out cooperation in science, education, culture, health and people-to-people exchanges. Our cooperation in all these fields has helped lay a solid popular and social foundation for pursuing the Belt and Road Initiative. Each year, the national government of China provides 10,000 government scholarships to participating countries of the Belt and Road Initiative, and its local governments have also set up special Silk Road scholarships to encourage international cultural and educational exchanges. A series of people-to-people exchange projects such as the Silk Road culture year and tourism year, art festivals, film and TV projects, seminars and think-tank dialogues have been introduced and conducted. These interactions and exchanges have brought our peoples increasingly closer.

These fruitful outcomes show that the Belt and Road Initiative responds to the trend of the times, conforms to the law of development, and serves the interests of the people. It surely has bright prospects.

Ladies and gentlemen,

Dear friends,

As we often say in China, "The beginning is the most difficult part." A solid first step has been taken in pursuing the Belt and Road Initiative. We should build on the sound momentum and steer the initiative towards greater success. In this regard, I would like to share with you my thoughts on how to advance the initiative for a better future:

First, we should build the Belt and Road into a road of peace. The ancient Silk Road thrived in times of peace, and declined in times of war. Without a peaceful and stable environment, it would be impossible to pursue the Belt and Road Initiative. We will foster a new model of international relations featuring mutually beneficial cooperation, and forge partnerships through dialogue instead of confrontation, and friendship rather than alliance. All countries should respect each other's sovereignty, dignity, territorial integrity, development path, social systems, and core interests, and accommodate each other's major concerns.

Some regions along the ancient Silk Road used to be "lands of milk and honey". Yet today, these places are often associated with conflicts, turbulence, crises and challenges. This state of affairs should not be allowed to continue. We should foster a vision of common, comprehensive, cooperative and sustainable security, and ensure that a security environment is built by all and for all. We should work to resolve flashpoint issues through political means, and promote mediation in the spirit of justice and fairness. We should intensify counter-terrorism efforts by addressing both symptoms and root causes, and by eradicating poverty, backwardness and social injustice.

Second, we should build the Belt and Road into a road of prosperity. Development holds the master key to solving all problems. In pursuing the Belt and Road Initiative, we should focus on the fundamental issue of development, release the growth potential of participating countries, achieve economic integration and interconnected development, and work for the benefit of all.

Industry is the foundation of an economy. We should deepen industrial cooperation so that the industrial development plans of different countries complement and reinforce each other. Focus should be put on major projects. We should enhance international cooperation in industrial capacity and equipment manufacturing, and seize the development opportunities presented by the new industrial revolution to foster new businesses and maintain dynamic growth.

Finance is the lifeblood of a modern economy. Only when the blood circulates smoothly can one grow. We should establish a stable and sustainable financial safeguard system that keeps risks under control. We should create new models of investment and financing, encourage closer cooperation between government and private capital, and build a diversified financing system and a multi-tiered capital market. We should also develop inclusive finance and improve financial service networks.

Infrastructure connectivity is the foundation of development through cooperation. We should promote land, maritime, air, and cyberspace connectivity, concentrate our efforts on key passageways, cities and projects, and connect networks of highways, railways, and sea ports. Since we have set the goal of building six major economic corridors under the Belt and Road Initiative, we should endeavor to meet it. We need to seize the opportunities presented by the new round of change in energy mix and the revolution in energy technologies to develop global energy interconnection and achieve green and low-carbon development. We should improve transregional logistics networks, and promote coordination in policies, rules, and standards so as to provide institutional safeguards for better connectivity.

Third, we should build the Belt and Road into a road of opening up. Opening up brings progress, while isolation results in backwardness. For a country to open itself to the outside world, it is like a silk moth breaking free from its cocoon. There will be short-term pains, but one gets a new life afterwards. The Belt and Road Initiative calls for opening up, which in turn will enable us to achieve both economic growth and balanced development.

We should build an open platform of cooperation, and uphold and foster an open world economy. We should jointly create an environment that is friendly to opening up and development, establish a fair, equitable and transparent system of international trade and investment rules, and boost an orderly flow of factors of production, efficient allocation of resources and full market integration. We welcome efforts made by other countries to foster an open economy in light of their respective national conditions, participate in global governance and provide public goods. Together, we will build a broad community of shared interests.

Trade is an important engine driving growth. We should embrace the outside world with an open mind, uphold the multilateral trading regime, advance the building of free trade areas, and promote liberalization of trade and investment. Of course, we should also focus on resolving issues such as imbalances in development, difficulties in governance, the digital divide and income disparity, and on making economic globalization open, inclusive, balanced and beneficial for all.

Fourth, we should build the Belt and Road into a road of innovation. Innovation is an important force powering development. The Belt and Road Initiative itself is new by nature, and its implementation needs to be driven by innovation too.

We should pursue innovation-driven development, intensify cooperation in frontier areas such as the digital economy, artificial intelligence, nanotechnology and quantum computing, and advance the development of big data, cloud computing, and smart cities, so as to turn them into a digital Silk Road of the 21st century. We should spur the full integration of science and technology with industries and finance, improve the environment for innovation, and pool resources for innovation. We should create space and build workshops for young people of various countries to cultivate entrepreneurship in this internet age and help realize their dreams.

We should pursue the new vision of green development and a way of life and work that is green, low-carbon, circular and sustainable. Efforts should be made to strengthen cooperation in ecological and environmental protection and build a sound ecosystem so as to realize the goals set by the 2030 Agenda for Sustainable Development.

Fifth, we should build the Belt and Road into a road connecting different civilizations. In pursuing the Belt and Road Initiative, we should ensure that, when it encounters different civilizations, exchange will replace estrangement, mutual learning will replace clashes, and coexistence will replace a sense of superiority. This will boost mutual understanding, mutual respect, and mutual trust between different countries.

We should establish a multi-tiered mechanism for cultural and people-to-people exchanges, and build more cooperation platforms and channels. We should boost educational cooperation, increase the number of exchange students, and improve the performance of cooperatively run schools. Efforts should be made to give think tanks a bigger role to play and establish think tank networks and partnerships. In the cultural, sports and health sectors, new cooperation models should be created to encourage projects for concrete results. Historical and cultural heritages should be fully tapped to jointly develop tourism products and protect heritage items in ways that preserve the distinctive features of the Silk Road. We should increase exchanges between parliaments, political parties and NGOs of different countries as well as between women, youth and people with disabilities, with a view to achieving inclusive development. We should also enhance international cooperation in the fight against corruption so that the Belt and Road will be a road of high ethical standards.

Ladies and gentlemen,

Dear friends,

China has reached a new starting point in its development endeavors. Guided by a vision of innovative, coordinated, green, open, and inclusive development, we will adapt to and steer the new normal in economic development, and seize the opportunities it presents. We will actively promote supply-side structural reform to achieve sustainable development, inject a strong impetus into the Belt and Road Initiative, and create new opportunities for global development.

– China will enhance friendship and cooperation with all countries involved in the Belt and Road Initiative on the basis of the Five Principles of Peaceful Coexistence. We are ready to share development experiences with other countries, but we have no intention of interfering in other countries'

internal affairs, or of forcing our social system and development model on others, and even less of imposing our own
will on others. In pursuing the Belt and Road Initiative, we
will not resort to outdated geopolitical maneuvering. What
we hope to achieve is a new model of mutually beneficial
cooperation. We have no intention of creating a small group
detrimental to stability; what we hope to create is a big family of harmonious coexistence.

– China has reached practical cooperation agreements
with many countries in relation to the Belt and Road Initiative. These agreements cover not only projects of hardware
connectivity, like transport, infrastructure and energy, but
also software connectivity, involving telecommunications,
customs and quarantine inspection. The agreements also
include plans and projects for cooperation in business and
trade, industry, e-commerce, maritime activities and green
economic development. The Chinese railway authorities will
sign agreements with their counterparts of relevant countries for further cooperation in China-Europe regular railway
cargo services. We will work to launch these cooperation
projects at an early date and see that they deliver early benefits.

– China will scale up financing support for the Belt and
Road Initiative by contributing an additional RMB100 billion
to the Silk Road Fund. We have encouraged financial institutions to conduct overseas Renminbi fund business with an
estimated amount of about RMB300 billion. The China Development Bank and Export-Import Bank of China will in-

troduce special lending schemes respectively worth RMB250 billion equivalent and RMB130 billion equivalent to support Belt and Road cooperation in the fields of infrastructure, industrial capacity and financing. We will also work with the AIIB, BRICS New Development Bank, World Bank and other multilateral development institutions to support Belt and Road-related projects. We will work with other parties concerned to formulate guidelines for financing Belt and Road-related development projects.

– China will endeavor to build a mutually beneficial business partnership with other countries participating in the Belt and Road Initiative, enhance trade and investment with them, and build a Belt and Road free trade network. These efforts are designed to promote growth both in our respective regions and globally. During this forum, China will sign business and trade cooperation agreements with over 30 countries, and enter into consultation on free trade agreements with related countries. Moreover, China will host the China International Import Expo starting in 2018.

– China will enhance cooperation in innovation with other countries. We will launch the Belt and Road Science, Technology and Innovation Cooperation Action Plan, which consists of the Science and Technology People-to-people Exchange Initiative, Joint Laboratory Initiative, Science Park Cooperation Initiative and Technology Transfer Initiative. In the coming five years, we will offer 2,500 short-term research visits to China for young foreign scientists, train 5,000 foreign scientists, engineers and managers, and set up 50 joint laboratories. We will set up a big data service platform for ecological and environmental protection. We will propose establishing an international coalition for green development on the Belt and Road, and we will provide support to related countries in responding to climate change.

– In the coming three years, China will provide assistance worth RMB60 billion to developing countries and international organizations participating in the Belt and Road Initiative to launch more projects to improve peoples' wellbeing. We will provide emergency food aid worth RMB2 billion to developing countries along the Belt and Road and make an additional contribution of US$1 billion to the Assistance Fund for South-South Cooperation. China will launch 100 "happy home" projects, 100 poverty alleviation projects and 100 healthcare and rehabilitation projects in countries along the Belt and Road. China will provide relevant international organizations with US$1 billion to implement cooperation projects that will benefit countries along the Belt and Road.

– China will put in place the following mechanisms to boost Belt and Road cooperation: a liaison office for the Forum's follow-up activities, Research Center for Belt and Road Financial and Economic Development, Facilitation Center for Building the Belt and Road, Multilateral Development Financial Cooperation Center in cooperation with multilateral development banks, and an IMF-China Capacity Building Center. We will also develop a network for cooperation among the NGOs in countries along the Belt and Road as well as new people-to-people exchange platforms such as a Belt and Road news alliance and a music education alliance.

The Belt and Road Initiative is rooted in the ancient Silk Road. It focuses on the Asian, European and African continents, but it is open to all other countries. Countries from all the five continents, Asia, Europe, Africa, North America and South America, can be partners of the Belt and Road Initiative. The initiative should be implemented through extensive consultation, and all should benefit from it.

Ladies and gentlemen,

Dear friends,

An ancient Chinese saying goes, "A long journey can be covered only by taking one step at a time." Similarly, there is an Arabic proverb which says that the pyramids were built by piling one stone block upon another. In Europe, there is also a saying which says, "Rome was not built in a day." The Belt and Road Initiative is a great undertaking which requires dedicated efforts. Let us pursue this initiative step by step, and deliver its achievements one by one. By doing so, we will bring true benefits to both the world and all its peoples.

In conclusion, I wish the Belt and Road Forum for International Cooperation every success.

Thank you.

Toast at the Welcoming Banquet for the Belt and Road Forum for International Cooperation

May 14, 2017

Your Excellencies heads of state, government and
    international organizations,
Distinguished guests,
Ladies and gentlemen,
Dear friends,

Good evening! On behalf of the Chinese government and people, my wife and myself, let me begin by warmly welcoming you to the Belt and Road Forum for International Cooperation.

To many of you, Beijing is not unfamiliar and may bring back many fond memories. As an ancient capital, Beijing has witnessed great historical changes over the centuries. It is also a modern city that has taken on a new look as China makes progress. More importantly, Beijing is an international metropolis where Eastern and Western civilizations meet and interact.

Here in Beijing, you may tour the time-honored Forbidden City, the Great Wall and the Temple of Heaven, or visit the modernistic "Bird's Nest", "Water Cube" and the National Center for the Performing Arts. You may choose to enjoy a performance of traditional Peking Opera or the typical Chinese comic cross-talk, or you can treat yourself to a Western-style ballet or symphony. You are likely to bump into trendy-looking Chinese youngsters in boutiques displaying international brands, or come across foreigners speaking fluent Chinese in the *hutong*, traditional alleys in local neighborhoods.

It is said you can see a world in a grain of sand and an ocean in a drop of water. Beijing's evolution from a tiny town to an international metropolis is just one example of how mankind progresses as people of different ethnic and cultural backgrounds interact in a common home and embrace a common future.

More than 2,000 years ago, our ancestors, driven by a desire for friendship, opened the overland and maritime Silk Roads, and thus started a great era of exchanges among civilizations.

Today, we are gathered here to renew the Silk Road spirit and discuss the Belt and Road development for international cooperation. This is both a continuation of our shared legacy and a correct choice for the future.

The Belt and Road Initiative embodies our aspiration for inter-civilization exchanges. As a vehicle that facilitates communication between different civilizations, the initiative will promote mutual learning and add splendor to human civilization.

The Belt and Road Initiative embodies our yearning for peace and stability. As a bond bringing countries closer to each other, the initiative will encourage solidarity, mutual respect and mutual trust between countries, and inspire our people to work together to build a harmonious and peaceful world.

The Belt and Road Initiative embodies our pursuit of common development. The initiative aims to break development bottlenecks, narrow development gaps and promote the sharing of development achievements among countries. It envisions a community of common development where we work together through thick and thin for a shared future.

The Belt and Road Initiative embodies our shared dream for a better life. The initiative weaves into a common vision the dreams of different countries and peoples. We will work to translate this vision into reality and deliver greater happiness and wellbeing to our peoples.

The High-level Dialogue of the Belt and Road Forum for International Cooperation held today has been a great success. The discussions were lively and the outcomes productive. Tomorrow, we will meet by Yanqi Lake for the Leaders Roundtable to jointly plan Belt and Road cooperation. We are at a fresh starting point, ready to embark on a new journey together.

It will be a journey full of hope. So long as we press ahead with a common vision without backpedaling or standing still, we will achieve greater connectivity and benefit from each other's development. Our common endeavor, just like the ancient Silk Roads, will have far-reaching impact and bring benefits to many generations to come.

Now please join me in a toast:

To the bright future of the Belt and Road;

To the development and prosperity of all countries;

To the full success of this Forum; and

To the health of all guests and your families.

Cheers!

New Beginning of Cooperation, New Dynamism for Development[*]

May 15, 2017

Dear heads of state and government,

Heads of international organizations,

I now declare open the Leaders Roundtable of the Belt and Road Forum for International Cooperation!

I welcome all of you to Yanqi Lake for the Leaders Roundtable. It gives us a good opportunity to discuss how to promote international cooperation for common prosperity.

I put forward the initiative of building the Silk Road Economic Belt and the 21st Century Maritime Silk Road in 2013. The initiative aims to promote infrastructure development and greater connectivity, align the development policies and strategies of individual countries, deepen practical cooperation, encourage coordinated and interconnected development, and bring about common prosperity.

I have come up with this Belt and Road Initiative based on my observation of and reflection on the world situation. We live in an age of major development, transformation,

---

* Opening speech at the Leaders Roundtable of the Belt and Road Forum for International Cooperation in Beijing.

and adjustment. A new round of scientific, technological and industrial revolution is in the making. New growth drivers are gaining momentum. National interests are increasingly entwined. Peace, development and mutually beneficial cooperation have become the trend of our times. On the other hand, the deep-seated problems in global development are yet to be addressed effectively. Global economic growth is not on solid ground. International trade and investment are sluggish. Economic globalization is encountering some headwinds. Development has become more uneven. And this is not to mention the other challenges that overshadow the world economy, like wars, conflicts, terrorism, and massive flows of refugees and migrants.

Confronted by these challenges, many countries are pondering the way forward, and have put forward many good development strategies and cooperation initiatives. However, in a world of growing interdependence and challenges, no country can tackle the challenges or solve the world's problems on its own. Individual countries need to coordinate national policies and make good use of economic factors and development resources on a greater global scale. Only in this way can we build synergy and promote worldwide peace, stability and common development.

The Belt and Road Initiative is rooted in history, but oriented towards the future. Reflecting our forefathers' aspirations for a better life, the ancient Silk Road connected nations in Asia and Europe, catalyzed cultural exchanges and mutual learning between the East and West, and made an important contribution to the progress of human civilization. We have every reason to draw wisdom and strength from the ancient Silk Road, advance cooperation in the Silk Road spirit of peace and cooperation, openness and inclusiveness, mutual learning and mutual benefit, and work together to build an even brighter future.

The Belt and Road Initiative originated in China but belongs to the whole world. It involves countries in different regions, at different development stages and with different cultures. It is a platform of open and inclusive cooperation, and a public product we jointly provide to the whole world. While the Belt and Road Initiative focuses on the Asian and European continents, it is open to all like-minded friends; it does not exclude or target any party.

In pursuing international cooperation and the Belt and Road Initiative, the parties concerned follow the principle of extensive consultation, joint contribution and shared benefits, and join hands to meet global economic challenges. Aiming to draw on each other's strength and deliver mutually beneficial results, the parties will explore new opportunities, seek new drivers and expand new space for development, moving closer towards a global community of shared future. This is what I had in mind when I first put forward the Belt and Road Initiative. It is also the ultimate goal of this initiative.

I am pleased to note that the global community has given positive responses and extensive support to the Belt and Road Initiative. More than 100 countries and international organizations participate in it. A large number of cooperation projects have been launched, and some are already in operation. An interconnected infrastructural network is taking shape. Industrial cooperation is gaining momentum. Policy coordination is improving. People are beginning to reap the benefits of Belt and Road cooperation, and feel even closer to each other.

All this provides a good basis for the Belt and Road Forum for International Cooperation. China has proposed and is hosting the Forum precisely for the purpose of extensive consultation on cooperation, joint contribution to the cooperation platform and shared benefits of cooperation by all the parties involved, to make sure that our peoples become better-off as a result of the Belt and Road Initiative.

At the High-level Dialogue yesterday, leaders of various countries and international organizations, and representatives of the business and academic communities offered many useful ideas and proposals, and many cooperation agreements were signed. I hope today's Roundtable will help us build more consensus, and chart the course and develop a blueprint for Belt and Road cooperation. I hope our discussions here will make good progress in the following areas:

First, setting the direction of mutually beneficial cooperation. Geese can fly a long way in safety through wind and storm because they move in flocks and help each other as a team. This brings home the message that the best way to meet challenges and achieve better development is through cooperation. In our cooperation, we need to work in a spirit of partnership, and follow the principle of extensive consultation, joint contribution and shared benefits. The building of policy, infrastructure, trade, finance and people-to-people connectivity should be our shared goal. We need to seek mutually beneficial results through greater openness and cooperation, avoid fragmentation, refrain from setting inhibitive thresholds for cooperation or pursuing exclusive arrangements, and reject protectionism. A peaceful and stable environment is required to pursue the Belt and Road Initiative. It is important for individual countries to step up cooperation, resolve their differences and disputes through dialogue and consultation, and work together to maintain regional security and stability.

Second, strengthening policy coordination and aligning our development policies and strategies. We need to improve policy coordination, and reject beggar-thy-neighbor practices. This is an important lesson that can be drawn from the global financial crisis and is still very relevant to the development of the world economy today. National development strategies are drafted in light of particular national circumstances, and have their own distinctive features. At the same time, they generally pursue the same goal. There is a great deal of common ground and complementarity among those strategies. We can make good use of this to promote and reinforce development for all of us.

Based on this common understanding, we need to set up a mechanism for policy coordination and mutual learning. We can build on it, work out plans for cooperation and take concerted actions to coordinate our plans, pursue interconnected development and share the benefits. We need to seek greater complementarity between Belt and Road cooperation and the implementation of the 2030 Agenda for Sustainable Development and the outcomes of the G20 Hangzhou Summit, the regional development initiatives of APEC, ASEAN, AU, EEU, EU and CELAC, and the development plans of relevant countries. By so doing, we will make the whole greater than the sum of its parts.

Third, deepening practical cooperation driven by concrete projects. As the saying goes, roads do not build themselves, and good things do not happen by themselves. Concrete action is the key to turning a blueprint into reality.

In terms of infrastructure connectivity, we need to push forward the construction of railways, roads and other major land transportation arteries, speed up the development of sea ports, and improve oil and gas pipelines, electricity transmission and telecommunication networks.

In terms of cooperation in the real economy, we need to vigorously develop economic corridors and work for the success of economic, trade and industrial cooperation zones to boost investment, industrial clusters and job creation, and take the path of innovation-driven development.

In terms of trade and investment liberalization and facilitation, we need to improve free trade areas, harmonize rules and standards, and provide a better business and institutional environment, so as to fully unlock the potential generated by greater connectivity.

In terms of financial cooperation, we need to broaden the channels, develop new models and reduce the cost of financing, and remove the bottlenecks that impede project implementation.

People-to-people exchanges are an important part of Belt and Road cooperation. We need to deepen cultural exchanges, make our cooperation more inclusive and solidly based, and enable the people to become the main drivers and beneficiaries in pursuing the Belt and Road Initiative.

Dear colleagues,

Yanqi Lake is an inspiring place with a rich history. It is a good place to start our journey of cooperation. Many people have compared the Belt and Road to a pair of soaring wings. Here from Yanqi Lake, let us spread our wings, soar to the sky, and reach out together for a future of peace, development and mutually beneficial cooperation!

Thank you.

Closing Remarks at the Leaders Roundtable of the Belt and Road Forum for International Cooperation

May 15, 2017

Dear colleagues,

As we have concluded our discussion at the last session, the Leaders Roundtable of the Belt and Road Forum for International Cooperation is coming to a close.

A shared commitment to friendship, cooperation and development has brought us together to this Forum in Beijing. In a warm, friendly and cordial atmosphere, we have had lively discussions on all agenda items. We shared policy practices and cooperation experience, envisioned the future, and put forward many good ideas and proposals.

One day may have been a bit tight for such a full agenda. But we have kept our discussions focused and pragmatic, and made them deep, broad and productive. In specific terms, I would say we reached broad consensus in the following aspects:

First, we stand ready to promote international cooperation on the Belt and Road development and jointly tackle challenges facing the global economy. Positive comments were made on the progress of Belt and Road cooperation.

It was agreed that, in the current global economic situation, the Belt and Road development is of high importance for fostering new drivers of growth, boosting internal drivers of growth and bolstering global growth, and will help make globalization more inclusive and beneficial for all. We will continue to work for greater progress in the Belt and Road Initiative to enhance policy, infrastructure, trade, financial and people-to-people connectivity.

Second, we support closer economic policy coordination and stronger synergy of our development strategies in an effort to achieve coordinated and interconnected development. There is a high degree of consensus on this point around the table. We all hope to form synergy among our policies and development programs through Belt and Road cooperation. We agreed to increase macro-policy coordination in the fields of economy, finance, trade and investment, and jointly foster a favorable external environment for development. We all back an open world economy, FTA building, and trade and investment liberalization and facilitation.

We hope to effectively synergize our national development strategies and the cooperation programs formulated by regional and international organizations to draw on each other's strengths and move forward side by side.

We all put a premium on innovation-driven development, and support closer cooperation in the frontier areas of cross-border e-commerce, big data, smart cities and low-carbon development to cultivate new industries, new forms and models of business, and tap new drivers of growth.

Third, we hope to translate consensus into action and achieve fresh outcomes in practical cooperation. We all believe that connectivity helps remove the bottlenecks hampering development, and hence is crucial for enhancing development momentum and improving the people's wellbeing. International cooperation on the Belt and Road Initiative should continue to take connectivity as a priority and be driven by major projects and programs. We need to advance cooperation in such areas as roads, railways, ports, aviation, oil and gas pipelines, electric power and telecommunications to build interconnected infrastructure networks.

We decided to vigorously pursue the building of economic corridors, economic cooperation zones and industrial parks, and advance cooperation in industrial capacity and equipment manufacturing to promote better and faster growth of the real economy. We all value investment and financing cooperation, support further mutual opening of financial markets and a greater role by development finance institutions, and endeavor to establish a solid financial safety net that is sustainable and risk-resilient.

Fourth, we hope to build bridges of people-to-people exchanges and deliver better lives to all our people. We regard the exchanges and mutual learning between civilizations along the ancient Silk Road as a valuable legacy, and believe that connecting the hearts of the people should be an integral part of Belt and Road international cooperation. We are ready to explore extensive people-to-people exchanges at all levels covering education, science, technology, culture, health, tourism and sports, and build more cooperation platforms and channels. We will actively create conditions to involve all communities and groups in this cooperation and make cultural exchanges diverse, interactive and broad-based. Responding to the people's expectations, we will enhance cooperation on environmental protection, climate change and the fight against corruption. We will also push forward visa facilitation to make people's travel easier and more enjoyable.

Fifth, we believe that the Belt and Road Initiative presents an open and inclusive platform for development in which all countries can participate, contribute and benefit as equals. In the spirit of inclusiveness, we will discuss and decide together on the basis of mutual respect and in keeping with the principle of extensive consultation, joint contribution and shared benefits. We will cooperate in an environment of ever-greater openness and seek mutually beneficial results through cooperation. The role of this Forum has received full recognition, and I wish to announce here that China will host the Second Belt and Road Forum for International Cooperation in 2019.

This Forum has also served as a platform for practical cooperation among the various parties. In the past couple of days, a host of cooperation agreements were signed, projects clinched and cooperation measures proposed. All these are reflected in a list of deliverables that will be released after the closing of the Forum. I believe these outcomes will lay a solid foundation for Belt and Road cooperation.

Dear colleagues,

People's pursuit of a better life has helped move history forward. Over 2,000 years ago, it was such a quest and an indomitable spirit that inspired our ancestors to open up the Silk Road linking Asia and Europe, contributing significantly to the advance of human civilization.

Today, the Belt and Road development is bringing together the peoples of all countries along the routes in a joint endeavor for common development and shared benefits through mutually beneficial cooperation. This is also what China's proposal for building a global community of shared future aims to achieve. As we work together to advance international cooperation on Belt and Road development, the ancient Silk Road will take on renewed dynamism. At this new starting point, we need to live up to our historical responsibility, be enterprising and take solid steps to make new progress in Belt and Road cooperation, and inject strong impetus into the building of a global community of shared future.

Before I conclude, I wish to once again express my appreciation to all of you. Thank you for your trust in me and the Chinese government, and for your strong support for the Chinese side as we prepared for and hosted the Forum.

Now, I declare the Belt and Road Forum for International Cooperation closed!

Follow a Path of Peaceful Development and Work to Build a Global Community of Shared Future*

October 18, 2017

The Communist Party of China strives for both the well-being of the Chinese people and human progress. To make new and greater contribution for mankind is our Party's abiding mission.

China will continue to hold high the banner of peace, development, cooperation, and mutual benefit and uphold its fundamental foreign policy goal of preserving world peace and promoting common development. China remains firm in its commitment to strengthening friendship and cooperation with other countries on the basis of the Five Principles of Peaceful Coexistence, and to forging a new form of international relations featuring mutual respect, fairness, justice, and win-win cooperation.

The world is undergoing major development, transfor-

---

* Part of the report to the 19th CPC National Congress, entitled "Secure a Decisive Victory in Building a Moderately Prosperous Society in All Respects and Strive for the Great Success of Socialism with Chinese Characteristics for a New Era".

mation, and adjustment, but peace and development remain the call of our day. The trends of global multi-polarity, economic globalization, IT application, and cultural diversity are surging forward; changes in the global governance system and the international order are speeding up; countries are becoming increasingly interconnected and interdependent; relative international forces are becoming more balanced; and peace and development remain irreversible trends.

And yet, as a world we face growing uncertainties and destabilizing factors. Global economic growth lacks energy; the gap between rich and poor continues to widen; hotspot issues arise often in some regions; and unconventional security threats like terrorism, cyber-insecurity, major infectious diseases, and climate change continue to spread. As human beings we have many common challenges to face.

Our world is full of both hope and challenges. We should not give up on our dreams because the reality around us is too complicated; we should not stop pursuing our ideals because they seem out of our reach. No country can address alone the many challenges facing mankind; no country can afford to retreat into self-isolation.

We call on the people of all countries to work together to build a global community of shared future, to build an open, inclusive, clean, and beautiful world that enjoys lasting peace, universal security, and common prosperity. We should respect each other, discuss issues as equals, resolutely reject the Cold War mentality and power politics, and take a new approach to developing state-to-state relations with communication, not confrontation, and with partnership, not alliance. We should commit to settling disputes through dialogue and resolving differences through discussion, coordinate responses to traditional and non-traditional threats, and oppose terrorism in all its forms.

We should stick together through thick and thin, promote trade and investment liberalization and facilitation, and make economic globalization more open, inclusive, and balanced so that its benefits are shared by all. We should respect the diversity of civilizations. In handling relations among civilizations, let us replace estrangement with exchange, clashes with mutual learning, and superiority with coexistence. We should be good friends to the environment, cooperate to tackle climate change, and protect our planet for the sake of human survival.

China remains firm in pursuing an independent foreign policy of peace. We respect the right of the people of all countries to choose their own development path. We endeavor to uphold international fairness and justice, and oppose acts that impose one's will on others or interfere in the internal affairs of others as well as the practice of the strong bullying the weak.

China will never pursue development at the expense of others' interests, but nor will China ever give up its legitimate rights and interests. No one should expect us to swallow anything that undermines our interests. China pursues a national defense policy that is in nature defensive. China's development does not pose a threat to any other country.

No matter what stage of development it reaches, China will never seek hegemony or engage in expansion.

China has actively developed global partnerships and expanded the convergence of interests with other countries. China will promote coordination and cooperation with other major countries and work to build a framework for major country relations featuring overall stability and balanced development. China will deepen relations with its neighbors in accordance with the principle of amity, sincerity, mutual benefit, and inclusiveness and the policy of forging friendship and partnership with its neighbors. China will, guided by the principle of upholding justice while pursuing shared interests and the principle of sincerity, real results, affinity, and good faith, work to strengthen solidarity and cooperation with other developing countries. We will strengthen exchanges and cooperation with the political parties and organizations of other countries, and encourage people's congresses, committees of the Chinese People's Political Consultative Conference, the military, local governments, and people's organizations to engage in exchanges with other countries.

China adheres to the fundamental national policy of opening up and pursues development with its doors open wide. China will actively promote international cooperation through the Belt and Road Initiative. In doing so, we hope to achieve policy, infrastructure, trade, financial, and people-to-people connectivity and thus build a new platform for international cooperation to create new drivers of shared development.

China will increase assistance to other developing countries, especially the least developed countries, and do its part to reduce the North-South development gap. China will support the multilateral trading regime and work to facilitate the establishment of free trade areas and build an open world economy.

China follows the principle of achieving shared growth through discussion and collaboration in engaging in global governance. China stands for democracy in international relations and the equality of all countries, big or small, strong or weak, rich or poor. China supports the United Nations in playing an active role in international affairs, and supports the efforts of other developing countries to increase their representation and strengthen their voice in international affairs. China will continue to play its part as a major and responsible country, take an active part in reforming and developing the global governance system, and keep contributing Chinese wisdom and strength to global governance.

Comrades,

The future of the world rests in the hands of the people of all countries; the future of mankind hinges on the choices they make. We, the Chinese, are ready to work with the people of all other countries to build a global community of shared future and create a bright tomorrow for all of us.

Seize the Opportunity of a Global Economy in Transition and Accelerate Development of the Asia-Pacific*

November 10, 2017

Chairman Vu Tien Loc,

Leaders of the APEC business community,

Ladies and gentlemen,

Dear friends,

Good afternoon! I am glad to come to Da Nang and meet all of you again.

Our region, the Asia-Pacific, has the biggest share of the global economy; and it is a major engine driving global growth. The business community is a primary contributor to growth, and it continues to explore new ways of thinking for development and put them into practice. That is why during the APEC Economic Leaders' Meeting over the past several years, I have always taken time to meet business leaders and discuss with you the approaches and measures we should take to address the challenges we face.

It has been 10 years since the international financial crisis

---

* Keynote speech at the APEC CEO Summit in Da Nang, Viet Nam.

broke out. Over the past decade, the international community has worked to steer the global economy back onto the track of recovery. Thanks to our efforts, the situation is improving. Despite risks and uncertainties, global trade and investment are picking up, people are more optimistic about the outlook of financial markets, and confidence is growing in all sectors.

Development is a journey with no end, but with one new departure point after another. An ancient Chinese philosopher once observed, "We should focus our mind on the future, not the past." We live in a rapidly changing world, and the global economy is going through profound change. We must therefore closely follow global economic trends, identify their underlying dynamics, keep to the right direction, and, on that basis, take bold actions.

– We are seeing a profound change in growth drivers. Countries are turning to reform and innovation to meet challenges and achieve growth. The potential of structural reform is being unlocked and its positive impact on growth has become more evident in various countries. A new round of technological and industrial revolution is gaining momentum. The digital economy and the sharing economy have registered rapid growth. New industries as well as new models and forms of business are flourishing. New growth drivers are being created.

– We are seeing a profound change in the model of global growth. As time passes, development takes on profound and richer implications. The vision of innovative, coordinated, green, open and inclusive development is gaining increasing support. To achieve more comprehensive, higher quality, and more sustainable development has become the shared goal of the international community. The need to implement the 2030 Agenda for Sustainable Development and adapt to climate change and other challenges of a global nature has become an important international consensus.

– We are seeing a profound change in economic globalization. Over the past few decades, economic globalization has made a significant contribution to global growth. Indeed, it has become an irreversible historical trend. Against the backdrop of evolving global developments, we face the need to make new adjustments to economic globalization in both form and substance. In pursuing economic globalization, we should make it more open and inclusive, more balanced, more equitable and beneficial to all.

– We are seeing a profound change in the system of global economic governance. The evolving global economic environment demands more from the system of global economic governance. We should uphold multilateralism, pursue extensive consultation, joint contribution, and shared benefits, forge closer partnerships, and build a global community of shared future. This, I believe, is what we should do for global economic governance in a new era.

Ladies and gentlemen,

Dear friends,

Faced with the profound changes in the global economy, should we, the Asia-Pacific economies, boldly lead reform and innovation, or hesitate and hold back? Should we steer economic globalization, or dither and stall in the face of challenge? Should we jointly advance regional cooperation, or go our separate ways?

This is my answer: We must advance with the times, live up to our responsibilities, and work together for a bright future of development and prosperity in the Asia-Pacific.

First, we should continue to foster an open economy and strive to achieve win-win outcomes. Openness brings progress, while self-imposed seclusion leaves one behind. We the Asia-Pacific economies know this too well from our own development history. We should put in place a regional cooperation framework that ensures consultation on an equal footing, wide participation and shared benefits. We should build an open Asia-Pacific economy and promote trade and investment liberalization and facilitation. We should guide economic globalization and make it more open, inclusive and balanced so that it benefits all countries and people of all social groups. We should proactively adapt to the evolving industrial division of labor across the world and actively steer reshaping of the global value chain so as to upgrade our economies and build up new strengths. We should support the multilateral trading regime and practice open regionalism to allow developing members to benefit more from international trade and investment.

To build a Free Trade Area of the Asia-Pacific (FTAAP) is the long-cherished dream of the business community in our region. It was in response to the call of the business community that APEC leaders, for the first time, initiated the FTAAP vision in Hanoi in 2006. In 2014, the FTAAP process was launched in Beijing. We should act to fully implement the Beijing Roadmap, move towards the FTAAP, and provide an institutional underpinning for an open economy in the Asia-Pacific.

Second, we should continue to pursue innovation-driven development and create new drivers of growth. The current global economic recovery is, to a large extent, the result of cyclical factors, while the lack of self-generating driving forces remains a nagging problem. To break free from the risk of a "new mediocre", the world economy must explore innovation as a new source of growth.

A new round of technological and industrial revolution is unfolding before us. The digital economy and the sharing economy are surging worldwide, and breakthroughs have been made in new technologies such as artificial intelligence and quantum science. We in the Asia-Pacific cannot afford to stand back and be onlookers. We should seize the opportunity, increase input in innovation, change the model of development, and nurture new growth areas. We should promote structural reform, remove all institutional and systemic barriers to innovation, and energize the market. We should implement the APEC Accord on Innovative Development, Economic Reform and Growth adopted in Beijing, extend cooperation on the internet and digital economy, and strive to be a global leader of innovative growth.

Third, we should continue to enhance connectivity and

achieve interconnected development. Interconnected development is the best way to achieve mutual benefit and win-win outcomes. We the Asia-Pacific economies are closely connected, and our interests are interlocked. Interconnected development will open up new horizons for our own development, and create a driving force for us all to achieve common development as partners. In 2014, the APEC Connectivity Blueprint was formulated. This blueprint should guide our efforts to build a comprehensive, all-round and multi-tiered Asia-Pacific connectivity network. We should boost the real economy through building connectivity, break through bottlenecks to development, and unlock potential. Through these efforts we can achieve coordinated and interconnected development.

In May this year a successful Belt and Road Forum for International Cooperation was held in Beijing. The Belt and Road Initiative calls for multi-party contribution and it has a clear focus, which is to promote infrastructure construction and connectivity, strengthen coordination on economic policies, enhance complementarity of development strategies, and boost interconnected development in order to achieve common prosperity. This initiative came from China, but belongs to the world. It is rooted in history, but is oriented towards the future. It focuses on the Asian, European and African continents, but is open to all partners. I am confident that the launch of the Belt and Road Initiative will create a broader and more dynamic platform for Asia-Pacific cooperation.

Fourth, we should continue to make economic development more inclusive and deliver its benefits to our people. The current headwinds hitting economic globalization stem largely from a lack of inclusiveness in development. Hard work is still needed if we are to bring the benefits of development to all countries and to all people throughout our societies, and thereby turn our vision into reality.

Over the past few years, we have actively explored ways to promote inclusive development and have built strong consensus around it. We should deepen regional economic integration, develop an open and inclusive market and strengthen the bonds of shared interests. We should make inclusiveness and sharing a part of our development strategies, improve systems and institutions to uphold efficiency and fairness, and safeguard social equity and justice. We should invest more in education, medical care, employment and other areas that are important to the lives of ordinary people, and address poverty and the widening gap between the rich and the poor. We should reach out to disadvantaged groups, improve the business environment for micro, small and medium-sized enterprises, and enable the workforce to better adapt to industrial transformation, so that all will have their fair share of opportunities and benefits.

Ladies and gentlemen,

Dear friends,

As an old Chinese saying goes, "A commitment, once made, should be delivered." Boosting development in the Asia-Pacific requires real action by all of us as members. As the world's second largest economy, China knows well its responsibility. Over the past five years, we have taken proactive steps to adapt to, manage and steer the new normal of China's economy, and extended supply-side structural reform. As a result, China's economy has maintained steady performance, and we are pursuing better-quality, more efficient, fairer and more sustainable development. Over the past four years, China's economy has grown by 7.2 percent on average each year, contributing over 30 percent of global growth. China is now a main driver powering global growth.

We have worked hard to remove systematic and institutional barriers that impede development through comprehensive reform. As many as 360 major reform initiatives and more than 1,500 reform measures have been taken. Breakthroughs have been made in key areas, and general frameworks for reform have been put in place in major sectors. We have accelerated efforts to build new institutions of the open economy and transform models of foreign trade and outbound investment to continue the shift from quantitative to qualitative improvement in trade.

We have advanced theoretical, practical, institutional, cultural and other innovations to unleash new impetus for growth. China has become a huge platform where all factors and players of innovation converge. From infrastructure to various economic sectors, from business models to ways of consumption, innovation is leading the way.

We have pursued a people-centered philosophy to make our development more inclusive and beneficial to all. Individual incomes have registered sustained growth, outpacing GDP growth for many years. Income gaps between urban and rural areas and between different regions have been narrowing, the middle-income group expanding, and the Gini coefficient dropping. More than 13 million new urban jobs have been created every year for the last four years. Significant advances have been made in pursuing green development, reduction in the intensity of energy consumption, and marked improvement in the ecological environment.

To lift all the remaining poor people out of poverty is a solemn commitment made by the Chinese government to the people. It is uppermost in my mind, and I have spent more energy on poverty reduction than anything else. Over the past five years, I have been to many poor areas in China to pin down the causes of poverty and address them in a targeted way. Decisive progress has been made in the fight against poverty. Over the past five years, more than 60 million people have shaken off poverty. The poverty headcount ratio has declined, and per capita rural incomes in poor areas have maintained double-digit growth. This has not come easily, and we are proud of what we have achieved in poverty reduction.

Ladies and gentlemen,

Dear friends,

China's development is an evolving historical process. Last month, the 19th National Congress of the Communist Party of China was successfully convened in Beijing. Responding to our people's desire for a better life, the Congress formulated a guide to action and a development blueprint for socialism with Chinese characteristics in the new era. It is envisaged that by 2020, China will turn itself into a moderately prosperous society in all respects, and by 2035, China will basically realize socialist modernization. By the middle of this century, China will become a great modern socialist country that is prosperous, strong, democratic, culturally advanced, harmonious and beautiful. Under the leadership of the CPC, the Chinese people will embark on a new journey.

First, this is a new journey of deeper reform across the board and unleashed dynamism for development. To resolve difficulties and problems on the way forward, we must extend all-round reform. We will focus more on solving problems, get rid of all outdated thinking and ideas and all institutional ailments, and break through the blockades of vested interests to inspire creativity and vitality throughout society. We will develop a set of complete institutions that are well-conceived, procedures-based, and efficient, and achieve modernization of China's system and capacity for governance. Next year, we will celebrate the 40th anniversary of China's launch of reform and opening up. China's reform will cover more areas; and more and stronger measures will be taken in pursuing this endeavor.

Second, this is a new journey of advancing with the times and exploring new models of development. China's economy is in a transition from a phase of rapid growth to a stage of high-quality development. We will be guided by a new development philosophy, put quality first, give priority to performance, and develop a modernized economy. We will pursue supply-side structural reform as our main task, work hard to achieve better quality and higher efficiency, and create more robust growth through reform. We will raise total factor productivity and accelerate the building of an industrial system that promotes coordinated development of the real economy with technological innovation, modern finance, and a talent pool. We will endeavor to develop an economy with more effective market mechanisms, dynamic micro-entities, and sound macro regulation. All these efforts will make China's economy more innovative and competitive. We will promote further integration of the internet, big data, and artificial intelligence with the real economy, and cultivate new drivers of growth in the digital economy, the sharing economy, clean energy and other areas. We will continue to explore new mechanisms and pathways for achieving coordinated development between regions, and promote the Coordinated Development of Beijing, Tianjin and Hebei, and development of the Yangtze River Economic Belt, the Xiong'an New Area, and the Guangdong-Hong Kong-Macao Greater Bay Area. We will build world-class city clusters and foster new sources of growth.

As China works hard to pursue innovation and higher quality of growth, new forms of business will keep emerging, more innovations will be used, and the development of different regions in China will become more balanced. All this will create a more powerful and extensive impact, present more opportunities for cooperation, and enable more countries to board the express train of China's development.

Third, this is a new journey towards greater integration with the world and an open economy of higher standards. China will not slow its steps in opening up. We will work together with other countries to create new drivers of common development through the launch of the Belt and Road Initiative. We will adopt policies to promote trade and investment liberalization and facilitation. We will implement the system of pre-establishment national treatment plus a negative list across the board, significantly ease market access, further open the service sector, and protect the legitimate rights and interests of foreign investors. All businesses registered in China will be treated as equals. We will grant more powers to pilot free trade zones to conduct reform, and explore the creation of free trade ports. We will speed up negotiations with partner countries on concluding free trade agreements and investment treaties, advance the FTAAP, work for the speedy conclusion of the Regional Comprehensive Economic Partnership negotiations, and endeavor to establish a global network of free trade areas.

In the next 15 years, China will have an even larger market and more comprehensive development. It is estimated that China will import US$24 trillion of goods, attract US$2 trillion in inbound direct investment, and make US$2 trillion of outbound investment. In November next year, China will hold the first China International Import Expo in Shanghai, which will provide a new platform for expanding cooperation in China's market with all parties.

Fourth, this is a new journey towards a better life for the people. To secure a better life for our people is what we aim to achieve in everything we do. We will ensure and improve living standards through development and meet people's ever-growing need for a better life. We will continue to promote social fairness and justice to see that our people will always have a strong sense of gain, happiness, and security. We will continue to implement targeted poverty alleviation and elimination measures and ensure that by the year 2020, all rural residents living below the current poverty line will have been lifted out of poverty. Each and every one of the 1.3 billion-plus people of China should lead decent lives. No one will be left behind.

We will speed up institutional reform for ecological conservation, pursue green, low-carbon and sustainable development, and implement the strictest possible system for environmental protection. By 2035, there will be a fundamental improvement in the environment; the goal of building a beautiful China will be basically attained. We will actively tackle climate change, and protect our common home for the sake of human survival. China's carbon dioxide emissions are expected to peak around 2030, and we will make every effort for such emissions to peak ahead of time. We will increase the share of non-fossil fuels in primary energy consumption to around 20 percent by 2030. Once we set a target, we will not relent in our efforts until it is met.

Fifth, this is a new journey towards a new type of international relations and a global community of shared future. Our dream as Chinese is closely connected with the dreams of the peoples of other countries. Our world is full of challenges and the road ahead will not be smooth. But we will not give up on our dream. We will redouble our efforts and work with all others to build an open, inclusive, clean, and beautiful world that enjoys durable peace, universal security, and common prosperity.

We Chinese believe that peace is priceless and that there should be harmony among all nations. We are committed to peaceful development and we will remain an anchor for peace and stability in the Asia-Pacific region and beyond. Guided by the principle of upholding the greater good and pursuing shared interests, China will actively develop global partnerships, expand the convergence of interests with other countries, and work to foster a new type of international relations featuring mutual respect, fairness, justice, and win-win cooperation. Acting on the principle of extensive consultation, joint contribution and shared benefits, we will be actively involved in reforming and developing the global governance system to make the international political and economic order more just and equitable.

Ladies and gentlemen,

Dear friends,

All of our people in the Asia-Pacific deserve peace, stability and prosperity; and all of us in the region should jointly deliver a bright future for the Asia-Pacific. A partnership based on mutual trust, inclusiveness, cooperation and win-win progress is what keeps our great Asia-Pacific family together and ensures the success of Asia-Pacific cooperation. Let us take solid steps to promote cooperation and usher in an even brighter future for the Asia-Pacific.

Thank you.

The Belt and Road Is an Important Platform for Promoting a Global Community of Shared Future*

December 1, 2017-May 15, 2018

I

In 2013, I proposed building a global community of shared future. I am delighted to see that friendly cooperation between China and other countries is expanding and the concept of a global community of shared future is gaining support and endorsement from a growing number of people and is turning from concept to reality.

My proposal of the Belt and Road Initiative is the practice of the concept. Over the past four years, the initiative has become a broad cooperation platform for countries keen to realize common development. Trickles converge into a sea, and the light of individual stars makes the Milky Way. I am convinced that as long as all parties embrace this concept and plan and practice together with persistent efforts, the

---

* Excerpts from three speeches.

goal of building a global community of shared future will be realized.

(from the keynote speech at the opening ceremony of CPC in Dialogue with World Political Parties High-level Meeting, December 1, 2017)

II

Five years ago, I put forward the Belt and Road Initiative. Since then, more than 80 countries and international organizations have signed cooperation agreements with China. The initiative may be China's idea, but its opportunities and outcomes are going to benefit the world. China has no geopolitical calculations, seeks no exclusionary blocs and imposes no business deals on others. It must be pointed out that as the Belt and Road Initiative is a new initiative, it is perfectly natural for there to be different views. As long as the parties embrace the principle of extensive consultation, joint contribution and shared benefits, we can surely enhance cooperation and resolve differences. This way, we can make the initiative the broadest platform for international cooperation in keeping with the trend of economic globalization and to the greater benefit of all our peoples.

(from the keynote speech at the opening ceremony of the Boao Forum for Asia Annual Conference 2018, April 10, 2018)

III

Since the 18th National Congress of the CPC in 2012, China has actively advanced innovations in diplomatic theories and practices, improved multi-faceted diplomacy, promoted the Belt and Road Initiative and advanced its implementation, and been deeply involved in reforming and building the global governance system. It has also firmly safeguarded national sovereignty, security and development interests, enhanced the centralized and unified leadership of the CPC Central Committee over foreign affairs, developed a distinctive diplomatic approach befitting its role as a major country, and achieved historic successes.

In the current world with more unpredictable and destabilizing factors, China faces both opportunities and challenges. We need to understand very clearly the changes in the international situation, recognize the trends of development in China and elsewhere along with the risks and challenges on the road ahead, take necessary precautions, and manage them properly. For now and in the years to come, we must further improve diplomatic planning, implement plans for major diplomatic activities, enhance our awareness of risks, and firmly safeguard national sovereignty, security and development interests.

The Belt and Road Initiative is an important platform for promoting a global community of shared future. In recent years the initiative has been transformed from idea to action. It has catalyzed concrete international cooperation and witnessed remarkable achievements. In order to promote the initiative we will effectively implement the results of the first Belt and Road Forum for International Cooperation held last May, win consensus from all sides, plan a vision for cooperation, open wider to the outside world, and enhance communication, consultation and cooperation with other countries, and bring more benefit to the people of all countries.

(from the speech at the first meeting of the Foreign Affairs Commission of the CPC Central Committee, May 15, 2018)

Forge a Route for Cooperation Across the Pacific*

January 22, 2018

The world is now at a stage of major development, transformation, and adjustment. All countries are interdependent and increasingly connected to each other, and humanity faces many common challenges. Although geographically distant, China and the Latin American and Caribbean states are all developing countries in pursuit of the common dream of world peace, prosperity, and a better life for our peoples. The Chinese people will work with the peoples of Latin America and the Caribbean in making a greater contribution to the building of a global community of shared future.

When I proposed international cooperation on the Belt and Road Initiative four years ago, China offered to work with all interested parties to build a new platform of global cooperation, to boost interconnectivity, and to add new drivers for common development. The initiative has received warm support from the international community, including

---

* Part of the congratulatory letter to the Second Ministerial Meeting of the Forum of China and the Community of Latin American and Caribbean States.

many Latin American and Caribbean countries. In ancient times Chinese ancestors braved the oceans and opened up the maritime Silk Road between China and Latin America. Today, as we roll out the blueprint for the Belt and Road Initiative, we strive to forge a route for cooperation across the Pacific, in order to draw closer the two lands of abundance of China and Latin America, and open a new era of friendly relations.

Let us sail together towards a better tomorrow for China and Latin America, and a better future for humanity.

Coordinate Development Strategies and Actions to Advance the Belt and Road Initiative*

July 10, 2018

Sino-Arab friendship is time-honored and strong as ever. The Chinese and Arab peoples, though far apart in distance, are close like a family. Our ancestors, merchants and diplomatic envoys alike, traveled back and forth along the overland and maritime Silk Roads. In the modern era, we fought side by side for independence and liberation. We also gave each other strong support in development, creating a splendid chapter of win-win cooperation. Past and present experiences have proven that whatever changes may take place in the world and whatever obstacles may confront us, China and Arab states have always been good partners, sharing mutual benefit, and good brothers, going through thick and thin together.

To facilitate the common prosperity and progress of interested countries, China has put forward the Belt and Road Initiative. With a commitment to the principles of extensive

---

* Part of the speech, titled "Joining Hands to Advance Sino-Arab Strategic Partnership in the New Era", at the opening ceremony of the Eighth Ministerial Conference of the China-Arab States Cooperation Forum in Beijing.

consultation, joint contribution and shared benefits, this initiative focuses on promoting policy, infrastructure, trade, financial and people-to-people connectivity. It has attracted wide support and active participation from the Arab world and the broader international community. As important participants and co-creators of the ancient Silk Road civilization located at the juncture of the land and maritime Silk Roads, Arab states are natural partners in Belt and Road cooperation.

Belt and Road cooperation features prominently in the Arab Policy Paper issued by the Chinese government. The Arab League Council at the level of foreign ministers has adopted a resolution expressing the collective political will of Arab states to participate in the Belt and Road Initiative. It is expected that later during this ministerial conference, a Declaration of Action on China-Arab States Belt and Road Cooperation will be signed.

Over the past four years, China and Arab states have worked together to develop Belt and Road cooperation in light of regional realities, combine collective action with bilateral cooperation, and promote development while upholding peace. Complimenting each other's strengths and pursuing win-win results, we have delivered benefits to people both in our region and beyond. As various projects attest, a dynamic situation has been created and many fruits harvested in our Belt and Road cooperation.

Also over the past four years, Belt and Road cooperation has energized every dimension of Sino-Arab relations and propelled all-round Sino-Arab cooperation into a new phase.

In this context, I am pleased to announce that after friendly consultation between the two sides, we have agreed to establish a Sino-Arab future-oriented strategic partnership of comprehensive cooperation and common development. This marks a new historical milestone in Sino-Arab friendship and cooperation.

As we advance the Belt and Road Initiative, China stands ready to work with the Arab side to coordinate our development strategies and actions. We must strive to uphold peace and stability in the Middle East, safeguard fairness and justice, promote common development, and learn from each other as friends do. This joint commitment will help us build a Sino-Arab community of shared future for China and Arab states – and one for all of humanity.

First, China and Arab states need to strengthen strategic trust. A Chinese adage has it that "a just world should be pursued for the common good". The Middle East faces the urgent task of removing the barriers to peace and resolving the development conundrum. People in the region yearn for peace and development. Having formulated its Middle East policy in line with such yearnings, China is an advocate of the legitimate concerns of Arab states in the international arena and stands ready to play a bigger role for peace and stability in the region.

We must stay committed to dialogue and consultation. The many intractable issues in the Middle East must be addressed by all stakeholders together. They should not and cannot be decided by one party alone. We need to uphold the principle of sovereignty and oppose division and fragmentation. We need to champion inclusive reconciliation and stand against forced compromises. We need to fight terrorism and take well-coordinated actions to improve people's lives.

China is ready for more dialogue and consultation with Arab states on a wide range of topics such as development for peace, collective security, humanitarian assistance, shipping corridors, and a nuclear-weapon-free zone. I hereby announce that China is setting up a special program for economic reconstruction through industrial revitalization. Under this program, a credit line of US$20 billion will be extended, in accordance with commercial principles, to projects that will produce good employment opportunities and positive social impact in Arab states that have reconstruction needs. China will provide an additional RMB600 million of assistance to the peoples of Syria, Yemen, Jordan and Lebanon to meet their humanitarian and reconstruction needs. China will also discuss with regional countries the implementation of programs totaling RMB1 billion to help interested countries build up capacity for maintaining stability.

Second, China and Arab states need to help each other realize dreams of rejuvenation. The Arab world is strategically located and blessed with abundant energy resources. With our strong complementarity and converging interests, China and Arab states must synergize our development strategies in pursuit of our respective dreams of rejuvenation.

In this effort, we must stay focused on connectivity. China

welcomes opportunities to participate in the development of ports and the construction of railway networks in Arab states, and support Arab efforts in building a logistics network connecting Central Asia with East Africa, and the Indian Ocean with the Mediterranean. We need to work together to build a maritime cooperation center to boost the ocean industry, enhance our ability to provide ocean-related public services, and create a "blue economy corridor". The two sides may jointly build a Belt and Road space information corridor, strengthen aerospace cooperation, and enable Arab states to access China's BeiDou Navigation System and meteorological satellite remote-sensing technology for the good of their national development.

China and Arab states need to boost cooperation in the oil and gas and low-carbon energy sectors, which are the main drivers of our energy cooperation. We will continue our "oil and gas-plus" model and intensify energy cooperation across the entire industrial chain, which includes oil and gas exploration, extraction, refinery, storage and transportation. In the meantime, given the surging global energy revolution and the boom in green and low-carbon industries, we need to work more closely on peaceful uses of nuclear energy and in the solar, wind and hydro power sectors. These efforts will lead to an energy cooperation structure which is underpinned by oil and gas and reinforced by nuclear and clean energy sectors. Based on this structure, we can build a strategic partnership in energy sectors that delivers mutual benefits and fosters long-term friendship.

Financial cooperation must go in tandem with cooperation in new and high technologies. We need to explore how best new and high technologies and financial services can facilitate our cooperation and provide short- and long-term support for the Belt and Road. To this end, we must find a model that suits the needs and conditions of the Middle East.

China supports the establishment of a financial platform for industrial cooperation. The platform is expected to offer access to diversified sources of funding for the development of industrial parks and provide an enabling environment for enterprises to grow in these parks through its financial support and other services. The Chinese government supports Chinese financial and securities institutions in partnering with Arab states' sovereign wealth funds and regulatory bodies to build an international trading platform that is based in the Gulf region, serves the Middle East and North Africa, and attracts investors from around the globe. This platform can be an enabler of Belt and Road cooperation by facilitating the free flow of production factors, efficient allocation of resources and deep integration of markets. To stimulate more exchanges and cooperation between financial institutions, China will set up a Sino-Arab inter-bank association and equip it with a credit line of US$3 billion.

In light of the medium- to long-term development plans followed by Arab states, China will pursue closer cooperation with Arab states in the digital economy, artificial intelligence, new materials, biopharma and smart cities. We need to fully implement our science and technology partnership program and build joint laboratories in key areas of mutual interest. We also need to accelerate our work on a cyber Silk Road, and strive for more cooperation, consensus, and outcomes in internet infrastructure, big data, cloud computing and e-commerce.

Third, China and Arab states need to achieve win-win outcomes. With a commitment to deeper reform in all areas, to continuing its fundamental policy of opening up, and to pursuing development with its doors wide open, China is expected to import over US$8 trillion of goods and make over US$750 billion of outbound investment in the next five years. This will bring more opportunities and real benefits to Arab states. We need to fully leverage special and concessional loans in support of industrialization in the Middle East, and encourage more Chinese business involvement in the development and operation of industrial parks in Arab states to boost industrial clusters there. China looks forward to the participation of Arab states in the first China International Import Expo in Shanghai this November, and in the course of the next five years China will invite all Arab states to the Expo and its Country Pavilion for Trade and Investment. China will work for solid progress in its FTA negotiations with the Gulf Cooperation Council and with Palestine, and stands ready to explore with more Arab states the possibility of concluding full-fledged free trade agreements.

Fourth, China and Arab states need to promote inclusiveness and mutual learning. A civilization stays vibrant through constant interactions with other civilizations. The Chinese and the Arab civilizations, sharing a long history of mutually reinforcing exchanges, have all the more reason to draw wisdom and strength from each other in this day and age. I am glad to note that the Sino-Arab Research Center on Reform and Development that I proposed is operating well as an intellectual platform for experience sharing on reform, opening up and governance. I wish the Center still greater success in providing more intellectual support to both sides.

We must spread the message of peace, harmony and truth. One way to do that is to make a continuing success of the Roundtable on Sino-Arab Inter-civilization Dialogue and Eradication of Extremism. Efforts should be made to clear up misunderstandings through dialogue, solve disagreements through tolerance, and foster a wholesome environment in which genuine faith and good deeds prevail. We need to delve deeper into different religions for ideas of greater harmony and positivity, and interpret religious teachings in light of the progressing times. It is important that we work together to cultivate a healthy cyber culture to oppose the spread of extremist content and hate speech through the internet.

To enhance mutual understanding between the Chinese and Arab people, China will do the following for Arab states in the coming three years: invite 100 young leaders in innovation, 200 young scientists, and 300 science professionals to workshops in China; invite 100 religious leaders and 600 political party leaders to China; provide 10,000 training opportunities; and send 500 medical staff to Arab states.

To this end, I am glad to announce the official launch of a Sino-Arab press center, a Sino-Arab e-library portal and the Fourth Arab Art Festival co-hosted by the two sides in China.

图书在版编目 (CIP) 数据

习近平谈"一带一路":英文 / 习近平著 . —— 北京:外文出版社 , 2019. 4
ISBN 978-7-119-11998-4

I. ①习… II. ①习… III. ①习近平 – 讲话 – 学习参考资料 –
英文② "一带一路" – 国际合作 – 学习参考资料 – 英文 IV. ① D2-0 ② F125

中国版本图书馆 CIP 数据核字 (2019) 第 067957 号

习近平谈"一带一路"

© 外文出版社有限责任公司

外文出版社有限责任公司　出版发行

（中国北京百万庄大街 24 号）

邮政编码：100037

http://www.flp.com.cn

环球东方（北京）印务有限公司印刷

2019 年 4 月（小 16 开）第 1 版

2019 年 4 月第 1 版第 1 次印刷

2019 年 8 月第 1 版第 3 次印刷

（英文）

ISBN 978-7-119-11998-4

12000（精）